Unwavering Hope

How I Found Strength in My Storm, Gratitude in My Grief and Joy in My Journey

Rhonda G. Mincey, M. Ed.

GREAT ONE PUBLISHING

Copyright © 2023 Rhonda G. Mincey
All rights reserved.

Under the U.S. Copyright Act of 1976, the scanning, uploading, and electronic sharing of any part of this book without written permission from the publisher constitutes unlawful piracy and theft of the author's intellectual property.

The advice and strategies contained herein may not be suitable for your situation. You should consult with a professional when appropriate. Neither the publisher nor the author shall be liable for any loss or damages, including but not limited to special, incidental, consequential, personal, commercial, or other damages.

Scriptures are from the Holy Bible, New International Version®, NIV®. Copyright © 1973, 1978, 1984, 2011 by Biblica, Inc.™ Used by permission of Zondervan. All rights reserved worldwide. The "NIV" and "New International Version" are trademarks registered in the United States Patent and Trademark Office by Biblica, Inc.™

For bulk copies of this book or speaking and media appearances by the author, contact:
Great Success, LLC
7 Venture Drive, Suite 104-116
Bluffton, SC 29910
www.rhondamincey.com

ISBN: 978-0-9882039-5-2

Proceeds from this book provide clean water and educational supplies to families in rural Africa. For information, please email: rhonda@rhondamincey.com

Printed in the United States of America

Dedication

To my late mother, Dorothy Zeigler, who holds a special place in my heart.

To my amazing husband, Doug, who has been my rock during my most challenging times.

To my readers and followers who need a word or two of encouragement.

Preface

Walking on the beach early one morning, I noticed the dark skies stretching across the Atlantic Ocean. But I didn't focus on its darkness since I knew it would soon give way to light. So, I waited, with childlike anticipation, for the beautiful sunrise to appear just beyond the horizon.

I stood there, my feet firmly planted in the sand, like a giddy schoolgirl, unable to keep my excitement in check. And looked wide-eyed as the sun rose, gradually lighting the skyline in vibrant reds, yellows, and oranges – a medley of Hope, like a kaleidoscope! *"Radiance is rising,"* I recall saying to myself. Can you imagine witnessing something this magnificent?

The sun continued to rise higher and higher, distracting me from the blackness that had only recently enveloped the earth.

This innocuous experience reaffirmed that something tremendous could arise from obstacles in your life – one moment, distress hovers over you, and then the next, you see brighter days ahead. My friends, this signifies the power of Hope.

> *Though darkness may overwhelm us, we all have choices: stay in that dark place and sulk. Or seek the light and soar.*

Rumi, a well-known 13th-century philosopher, declared, "There is hope after despair and many suns after darkness."

Contrary to popular belief, Hope isn't a genie in a bottle. Nor will it miraculously heal you or your loved ones.

So what is hope? Let's look at some ways Merriam-Webster defines Hope:

- Desire accompanied by expectation of fulfillment (I came in hopes of meeting you)

- Someone or something on which hopes are centered (My only hope for success)

- Something desired or expected (I have great hopes for the coming year)

According to these definitions of Hope, what you wish for may happen, but it isn't guaranteed.

In contrast, the Bible provides us with a different definition of Hope. *Hebrews 11:1* states, "Now faith is the substance of things hoped for, the evidence of things not seen."

What does this mean exactly? It's simple. It means Hope is a confident expectation – it never implies maybe or if. For example, you confidently expect the sun to rise in the East and set in the West, not vice versa. Likewise, you confidently expect to achieve your God-given purpose in life.

Considering this, you must search for Hope. Once you find it, seize it! Because if you can grasp it, you can find the will and way to depart the darkness, leaving the fog and funk behind, and reach your destiny.

Like the sun, you rose this morning, so you have a reason to Hope! That's right. A new day is dawning! Therefore, let's embrace it with open arms, sincere appreciation, and great anticipation.

Ready?

Epigraph

By: Rhonda G. Mincey

A Brighter Day

What do you do when life blindsides you?
Do you hold on? Lose it? Push? Pursue?
When your situation seems dire and bleak,
Your heart is heavy, but your will is weak.
How do you move past the pain?
How do you maintain? Step up? Stay sane?
In the darkest of times, when you're on your knees,
God's attentive ears are attuned to your pleas.
Through your fears and falling tears.
God is still there. God cares. God hears.
So lift your head high. Dry your eyes.
For this did not catch God by surprise.
God will bring you back from the brink.
His loving arms will not let you sink.

Through ominous skies and pelting rain,
God commands the sun to rise again.
To give you a glimpse, a glimmer of hope,
That strengthens you so you can cope.
So you, too, can rise and firmly stand,
Though the ground may seem like sand.
For you are re-si-li-ent.
You are *built* and *equipped* for this!
So pause. Breathe. Trust. Pray.
A brighter day is on the way.

Acknowledgements

I'm forever indebted to my family and the medical staff who cared for my mom during her illness.

I want to give special thanks to Barbara, Charlie, and my grief support family for providing a safe space for me to heal.

Lastly, I thank my ambassadors for helping me spread hope by promoting this book.

Proceeds from this book help support the nonprofit Hope Springs Africa.

Contents

Introduction	XV
1. Searching For Answers	1
2. Sending Out an SOS	7
3. Staying Afloat	13
4. Pressing Forward	33
5. Turning Your Pain into Gain	49
6. Reaching Your Destiny	61
7. Empowering Lives	71
8. Trading Places	95
9. Marching Orders	105
About the Author	111
Also By	113

Introduction

I sat in the car several times with tears flowing down my cheeks. I recall the pain I felt while crying in my doctor's parking lot after he told me again that I wasn't pregnant despite spending thousands of dollars on infertility treatments and enduring painful shots. My agony seemed endless.

Many years later, after visiting my son in jail, I drove home, my chest in my throat. As I labored to breathe, I couldn't help but ask myself: *What went wrong?* With no satisfactory answer to my pressing question, I struggled to find solace during this humiliating and disappointing time.

And I can never forget sobbing on the way home from the hospital after visiting my mom as her health rapidly deteriorated. I loved and adored her. After all, she fought to bring me into this world by getting a second opinion, which resulted in my birth! I felt devastated knowing she didn't have much longer to live. The anguish of my despair nearly paralyzed me.

The hard truth is that everyone will experience earth-shattering moments if they live long enough. So, our singular challenge is pressing forward toward our God-given purpose despite any pain, setbacks, and disappointments. In other words, do not allow life's circumstances to defeat you.

All my misfortunes could have left me feeling depressed and deflated. But guess what? I'm still standing and moving ahead, living with purpose and promise.

***

I've kept pushing forward through unplanned, unfathomable, unprecedented agony, loss, and anguish.

***

I've also decided to turn my tragedies into triumphs, refusing to let my pain be in vain. For example, I completed this book requiring significant physical and emotional effort. I also rediscovered my passion for motivating women to shoot for the stars, which resulted in my International Women's Empowerment Conference in Africa and Asia. And I started a nonprofit organization, Hope Springs Africa, to transform the lives of disadvantaged families in the rural villages of Rwanda, Africa, by providing clean drinking water, educational supplies, and feminine hygiene products.

***

I'm walking in my purpose with a sense of urgency and newfound joy. And so can you, regardless of your circumstances!

***

Now, I don't claim to have the answers to life's hard questions. But I can offer you some wisdom based on my experiences. "Unwavering Hope" encourages and empowers you to:

- Embrace Hope during hard times.

- Cultivate faith as a source of strength.

- Navigate the journey of grief.

- Count your blessings.

- Develop resistance for the long haul.

- Count your blessings and pay it forward.

I've done the work and ask you to take it from someone with the battle scars to prove it.

You see, the classes I taught my students as a Human Services Professor couldn't heal the hurt my heart felt during difficult times. And even though I took notes in church and shouted "Amen!" with enthusiasm and conviction, the sermons my pastor preached didn't seem to register during my dark hours. Real talk: No amount of hype, high-fives, or "Halleluiahs" kept me going.

However, Hope pulled me through – Hope for both the present and future. And because of that, I look at it differently. H.O.P.E.™ – **H**ealing, **O**pportunity, **P**urpose, and **E**mpowerment™ – has now become the cornerstone of my goals and the principles that I live by. Based on my new perspective, I penned this book *Unwavering Hope: How I Found Strength in My Storm, Gratitude in My Grief, and Joy in My Journey.*

This book is the ultimate approach to staying strong and overcoming life's most pressing problems. It shares inspirational personal stories from me and others, the *"Heroes of H.O.P.E.*™,*"* everyday people who faced challenges and made difficult decisions that significantly impacted themselves and others.

To all my followers, you will notice that I am more transparent about my relationship with the Lord in this book than in previous books. Sure, I've shared God's love, grace, and faithfulness with people in my close circle, strangers on the street, and random people in a restaurant. However, because the world is hungry for Hope, begging for something better, and starving for sustenance, I felt compelled to share my testimony about how God has shown up in my life, delivering me through some of the most challenging times I've faced.

Unwavering Hope is more than a memoir. It will elevate your thinking and broaden your horizon, offering tried-and-true strategies not to allow life to get the best *of* you but to bring out the best *in* you. It's also a road map to help you hold on to Hope, fight for your faith, and reach for resilience as if your life (or the life of someone else) depended on it.

As a free resource to help you delve deeper into each chapter, I created the *Unwavering Hope* Companion Workbook as a companion piece to this book. Download it at rhondamincey.com. If you prefer a physical copy instead of a digital one, you can purchase it online.

Remember, passive thinking will get you nowhere, but purpose-driven action will springboard you to success. Therefore, make up your mind to apply the principles of this book to your life.

With that being said, if you want to live a powerful, peaceful, and purposeful life, let's look at Hope in a whole new way.

Chapter 1
Searching For Answers

"Asking 'Why,' can lead to understanding..." ~Daniel H. Pink

Life has a knack for throwing difficulties in our path when we least expect them. Personal challenges, professional setbacks, or unforeseen events can all leave us feeling overwhelmed and insecure. However, there is an often-overlooked tool that can help us navigate through the chaos: the simple act of asking, "Why?" Most of us have probably questioned something along the lines of:

- *Why me?*

- *Is God putting me through a test?*

- *Is this a problem that I created?*

- *Is this punishment for something I did?*

- *What have I done to deserve this?*

- *What caused this to occur?*

Have you asked any of those questions? I certainly have. When confronted with adversity, our instinct is to examine our situation, searching for an explanation and meaning. "Why?" prompts introspection and contemplation, resulting in clarity, perspective, and the strength to move forward. Let's explore.

To begin, asking "Why?" helps us understand our experiences. It compels us to look into the fundamental causes and factors that have led to our current situation. We now better understand ourselves, our behaviors, and any external variables that may have contributed. This self-awareness allows us to accept responsibility for our actions, learn from our mistakes, and progress.

Furthermore, asking "Why?" yields a more significant perspective. It lets us see beyond our immediate surroundings and consider the big picture. Although the solutions are sometimes unclear, questioning allows us to discover alternative ideas and possibilities. This broader viewpoint can result in significant insights, new concepts, and a renewed sense of purpose.

The question "Why?" might assist us in finding our fundamental motivations and ideals. It causes us to face our fears, Hopes, and dreams. We can reconnect with what truly matters to us by delving into the underlying reasons for our problems. This contemplation allows us to concentrate on our goals, make better decisions, and find the fortitude to persevere.

Finally, asking "Why?" can help to foster resilience and empowerment. It compels us to take control of our situations and actively seek solutions. We exercise our creativity and ingenuity by questioning our constraints and challenging the status quo.

This adjustment in perspective enables us to approach obstacles more proactively, design new ways to overcome them, and grow stronger.

However, it is vital to note that asking "Why?" does not give a simple cure for all problems. At times, answers can be disappointing or elusive. For example, you may understand that your poor decisions have brought you to where you are, leaving you feeling regret. Or you may not receive any revelation about what to do; instead, you hear crickets. And that's fine.

Remember that we cannot understand everything in life. But the good news is accepting uncertainty and acknowledging that we may not have all the answers may be humbling and transformative.

***

While searching for answers is beneficial, expending excessive energy to figure out why something happened is worthless since certain situations are so complex that even the brightest or most tuned-in individual cannot understand them. Moreover, if you keep overthinking and rationalizing, you will remain in the stormy season and miss the lesson.

***

I won't profess to know the answer to the question, "Why?" But I know God is sovereign; nothing about my past, present, or future shocks God (Acts 4:24). The same goes for you.

God has a unique plan for your life. He desires to prosper and not harm you, to give you Hope and a future (Jeremiah 29:11). God can use all your heartbreaks, disappointments, and tragedies for His glory. So, trust Him with your life.

Is this tough to understand? Yes! Would you rather avoid the pain? There is no doubt about that! But here's the reality: many aspects of God's character are beyond comprehension to our human intellect, no matter how hard we try. God says about our thoughts and actions in comparison to His:

"My thoughts are not your thoughts; neither are your ways my ways. As the heavens are higher than the earth, so are my ways higher than your ways and my thoughts than your thoughts" (Isa. 55:8-9).

This scripture reassures me that God reigns over me and the world when I want to pout or wallow in self-pity. Furthermore, it prompts me to view my circumstances differently.

For instance, I trust that God is with me despite feeling alone. As a result, I seek Him more in the quiet times. Second, my challenge serves as either a lesson or a blessing, making it a win-win situation. So, instead of only questioning, "Why?" I also ask:

- *"What do You want me to learn?"*

- *"What exactly do You want me to do right now?"*

- *"How can You use this to glorify You?"*

***

I fully believe that God entrusts me to handle the situation. As a result, I will get to the other side.

***

And guess what? The more I let go of my emotions and place my confidence in God, the better my predicament appears.

So, when faced with difficulties, searching for explanations offers several benefits. It allows us to make sense of our experiences, gain perspective, uncover our values, and grow as people. Additionally, we can manage our problems with better clarity, purpose, and the possibility of personal improvement when we question, "Why?"

The bottom line is this: Next time you face an obstacle, turn it into an adventure and opportunity for self-discovery and perseverance.

Chapter 2

Sending Out an SOS

"The dignity of human nature requires that we must face the storms of life." ~Mahatma Gandhi

Storms, which are naturally occurring destructive phenomena, affect people worldwide. Blizzards, for example, are common in Canada and Antarctica. Similarly, hurricanes routinely affect Bermuda, and monsoon rains are widespread in Asia. But, regardless of where you live, one thing is sure: Everyone will experience at least one storm.

Let's look at a storm's characteristics. Some storms are entirely unpredictable. They can catch you off guard by appearing out of nowhere and giving you little time to react. As a result, you panic because you are unprepared.

Conversely, other storms warn you. You see dark clouds or hear high winds, giving you time to take cover and mitigate the damage. As a result, you tend to cope better with these types.

We will encounter both natural and personal storms. For example, hurricanes come from Mother Nature. They can uproot trees, break power lines, and wash away homes, displacing people and destroying businesses.

Conversely, personal storms, like sickness and divorce, can devastate individuals, destroy relationships, derail dreams, jeopardize joy, and hijack Hope.

But here's the thing: Regardless of the storm, you must have unflinching resolve that you will get through it, irrespective of whether:

- You're the mother of a ten-year-old boy killed in a senseless school shooting.

- You're a husband and father whose boss informed you that the company you gave the past 15 years of your life to no longer requires your skills.

- You're a committed partner whose significant other has abandoned you for someone else.

- You're caring for someone you love whose health is declining.

- You receive a devastating medical diagnosis.

The list could go on and on. However, regardless of the challenge, you need an anchor to hold you steady until assistance arrives. If not, the storm can *shipwreck* you and not *shape* you. Here's what I mean: The nature of the storm matters less than how you navigate through it. Navigation represents our actions and attitudes. While adversities in life are inevitable, our response and approach directly affect the outcome.

For example, I felt like I was in a never-ending downpour when dealing with my mother's health concerns. For seemingly an eternity, dark clouds of gloom loomed over my head. As my mother's health deteriorated, I was there for her 24 hours a day, seven days a week. This responsibility began to wear on me, and I felt ill-equipped to bear it with my strength, but I didn't know what to do.

In great distress, I needed a flare to fire into the air so that somebody could notice it and hurry to my rescue. Without it, I prayed, pleading with the only One who could calm the roaring waves and soothe my worried spirit. Until then, I did the best I could.

On one occasion, while caring for Mom, I desperately looked for an online teaching position to give me an outlet and generate an income. I'd invested significant money in my business but had to put it on hold suddenly.

While praying about this, I felt it was not the right time to work despite the circumstances. Instead, God put it on my heart that I was in a *season of service*. I then remembered God can *redeem*, *reward*, and *restore* us in ways we can't imagine (Job: 10-17). With a new perspective and feeling peaceful and no longer panicked, I ended my job search, and spent valuable time with Mom.

***

It's natural to lose perspective when focusing solely on the storm. We don't consider that what we call a hard time could be a gold mine.

***

Allow that to soak in for a moment. In other words, what you count as a blunder could be a blessing. Can you think of a time when you went through something difficult and were thankful you did? For example, maybe you were upset after a breakup but then met your soul mate. Perhaps you didn't get the job you wanted, so you had to "settle' for something else, not knowing your detour would lead you to your destiny. Are you following me? Then stick with me, and let's go a little further. I need your full attention because what I say next is good stuff! Ready?

Your "SOS" – a Morse code international distress signal used by ships – might not mean you're in distress. Nor is your "SOS" always a test. Instead, your "SOS" could have a deeper meaning. For example, while you are going through difficulty, grief, or suffering, there may be more to it below the surface. Let's dive in.

- Do you need to get outside your comfort zone to reach the next level?
  You could be in a *Season of Strengthening*.

- Do you need to calm the noise around you and pause to hear what God wants to say to you?
  You might be in a *Season of Silence*.

- Do you want to be alone with God to immerse in His presence?
  You might be in a *Season of Solitude*.

- Do you spend considerable time caring for a loved one, leaving little time for yourself or your job?
  You could be in a *Season of Service*.

- Do you need to relinquish control of your plans and priorities?
  You could be in a *Season of Surrender*.

- Do you accept a mediocre existence and refuse to believe God for something significant?
  You could be experiencing a *Season of Stretching*.

- Do you need to discover your gifts and how to use them for God's glory?
  You might be going through a *Season of Soul-Searching*.

- Is it time to change your old habits, ideas, and occupations to become healthier and happier?
  You may be in a *Season of Shifting*.

It may take some time to figure out which season you are in. However, changing your perspective during difficult times, as I did, is immensely helpful. Although storms, like life, are unpredictable, knowing these concepts gave me a new feeling of serenity and an inner drive to stay the course.

***

Whatever storm you're in, take heart, for there's good news: Like seasons, storms don't last forever.

***

So hold your head up, believing this, too, shall pass! Now name your problem and declare, by faith, that you will come out stronger.

This _____ won't get the best of me! My situation won't *define* me. Instead, it will *refine* me!

Now, take the necessary steps to make it happen because faith does not develop passively but through deliberate and determined action. Remember, *"Faith without works is dead" (James 14-18).*

We must progress from proclamation to manifestation, surviving the storm to thriving. Let's do this.

Chapter 3

Staying Afloat

"Rest, but never quit. Even the sun has a sinking spell each evening. But it always rises the next morning. At sunrise, every soul is born again." ~Muhammad Ali

Staying afloat during hard times means remaining resilient and pushing forward despite facing challenges or adversities. It's about maintaining one's emotional and mental balance, not succumbing to overwhelming pressures, and finding ways to cope and adapt in the face of difficulties.

Recall a hard place in your life that you made it through – nothing traumatic or recent because the goal is not to conjure up painful memories or reflect on an event where healing is still occurring. Instead, this is like a celebration of sorts, remembering your victory. Which one came to mind? Think about what happened and how you dealt with it for a minute.

Did you go through the motions of "doing life" robotically as the storm raged around or inside you? Did your everyday life come to a halt when the crisis arrived? Did you force yourself out of bed? Did you turn to friends or a higher power?

How did you overcome your adversity or heartbreak? Was it easy to get to where you are today? If I'm correct, you're probably thinking, *Rhonda, are you kidding me?* Listen, I get it.

Maintaining your sanity can require a significant amount of effort when trouble shows up. After all, while some people pull *for* you, other things pull *against* you. So you're torn, trying to be everything to everyone while you need care and comfort.

***

But the good news is that during these trying times, God's grace becomes your lifeline, and His mercy your life vest that keeps you afloat. Though you may tread water or even gulp it at times, you don't panic, knowing that help is coming.

***

Until that time comes, what do you do? How do you sustain yourself until what you've been dreaming of and believing in shows up? After looking back on how I got through difficult times, I discovered that proper preparation and application are critical to weathering any storm.

Therefore, I compiled the following 12 strategies that helped me stay afloat.

1. Look for the Silver Lining

When the world seems black and bleak,
the weight of our worries makes us weak,
and the sun seems to play hide-and-seek,
the silver lining we must seek.

What does the phrase "the silver lining" suggest to you? During the Covid-19 pandemic, experts recommended we look for the proverbial silver lining. But what exactly does that mean, and how do we find it?

The silver lining is like a gray cloud with a bit of light peeking through. It is an optimistic viewpoint that something positive can come from a negative situation. So, when you look for the silver lining, you look for the bright side, the upside. Doing so gives you a grateful heart and a glimmer of optimism.

Here's a real-world example. When my mother was diagnosed with lung cancer, our lives changed instantly. Mom needed round-the-clock care, so I dropped everything, left my home, and moved in with her.

But, despite this unexpected life-changing diagnosis, I found several bright spots:

- I worked for myself so I could move and work when I wanted.
- I had my husband's fantastic and unyielding support, who stepped up by caring for my mom and me.
- I visited Mom in the hospital and hospice despite Covid-19 restrictions.

As a result, I felt blessed.

So, how about you? What silver linings do you see when you remember a difficult time?

2. Receive Uplifting Words

When someone you care about or respect speaks to you, their words can thrust you onward or crush you to the core because their opinion matters to you.

It's like a self-fulfilling prophecy, which occurs when our (or someone else's) beliefs and expectations influence our actions.

For instance, I'll never forget my former boss telling me he could see me running a million-dollar nonprofit. His encouragement pushed me to start not one but two charity organizations: Made 2B More and Great Youth, Inc., serving hundreds of students and awarding scholarships.

On the flip side, when someone close to me commented on my appearance in a way that did not uplift me, I chose not to take their critique to heart, silently saying, *I do not receive that.*

3. Challenge Your Inner Critic

It's natural to blame ourselves when we're in a dark place. Of course, we don't intend to do so, but negative thoughts slip in, assaulting and insulting us before we realize it.

While admitting our shortcomings is beneficial, it's hurtful if we condemn ourselves. Criticizing thoughts can take root, becoming bitter fruit. To illustrate, I've occasionally had negative thoughts that astonished me to the point that I wondered where they came from! They weren't loud voices frightening me but damaging and distracting ideas in my mind.

Fortunately, I've learned how to deal with them with time and practice. Like a skilled lawyer, I *acknowledge* them. Then, I *analyze* them. Next, I *interrogate* them. Last, I have my closing argument.

Here are some examples:

- *"I am a failure"* changes to *"My past does not define me. I am a victor."*

- *"I'm going to have a nervous breakdown"* transforms into *"I'm mentally strong."*

- *"I can't get clients"* changes to *"I attract my ideal clients."*

- *"This is so difficult"* becomes "I am stronger than I realize."

- *"My life stinks"* transforms into *"My life is full of purpose and promise."*

Remember, judgmental thoughts count on us to hand over our power, but we have a choice. So, let us think positively and eliminate negative self-talk that undermines our success.

4. Look After Your Temple

We only have one masterfully created body. Looking after it during stressful or challenging times protects our physical health and supports our mental and emotional well-being, equipping us to navigate difficulties more effectively. Yet, we put our health on the back burner when facing hard times. The good news is we can restore it. Here's how:

A. Pay Attention to Your Diet

When under chronic stress, we may overeat, consuming a pint of ice cream or a box of doughnuts in one sitting. Or we may eat nothing, using adrenaline as fuel. Can you relate?

While taking care of my mom, I seldom ate. Thankfully, my friends Jennifer and Val helped me by reminding me to eat and bringing home-cooked food. Even so, consumed by things to do and something I couldn't control, I lost 10 pounds. While many individuals would gladly switch places with me, being slim, I didn't want to lose weight.

While initially concerned, I decided to view my unexpected weight loss as a cleansing – a way to remove negative energy, toxic thoughts, stress, and unhealthy fat. Also, here's the silver lining: I now had the opportunity to refresh emotionally and physically. So, instead of squandering this opportunity, I aggressively retook control of my health.

You, too, may change your eating habits for the better, even if you are going through challenges, by doing the following:

- Put snacks like nuts, seeds, and cheese in a baggie to keep them available. Peanut butter with apple slices, Greek yogurt with berries, and hummus with celery are also inexpensive and healthy options.

- Forgo processed, packaged, and junk foods. Choose fresh fruits, vegetables, lean meat cuts, poultry, and seafood.

- Eat home-cooked meals. A friend or family member might enjoy preparing dinner for you.

- Avoid skipping meals, particularly breakfast, because it gives you energy for the day.

- Drink plenty of water throughout the day for hydration. Include fruit to enhance the taste and add nutrients.

- Set reminders to eat and drink. It's easy to forget to eat or not have an appetite when stressed.

- Eat slowly and mindfully, taking in the sensations and flavors of each bite.

While some planning is needed, being intentional is the key to gaining the nourishment and strength you need. If this is too much for you to do, ask someone to help you.

B. Exercise

A healthy, active lifestyle energizes, motivates, and strengthens you, especially when the world's weight is on your shoulders. Aerobic workouts, like dance or jump rope, reduce stress-inducing hormones like cortisol, leaving you feeling confident, cheerful, and hopeful. On the other hand, strength training, like pull-ups or push-ups, can help with weight management, which stress can affect. Plus, they are simple and free.

Incorporating aerobic workouts and strength training exercises into your routine can provide a holistic approach to managing stress. Not only do they offer several physical benefits, but they also provide psychological benefits that can help you cope with and reduce feelings of anxiety.

What daily exercise will you begin to reduce stress and enhance your energy?

C. Breathe

Over the past years, I've grown more conscious of how I breathe. For instance, I'd hold my breath or exhale through my lips during stressful situations. I needed a "Woosah" moment to get my bearings. *Just breathe, Rhonda*, I'd think to myself. Then, my body would relax.

When you are stressed, you breathe short, quick breaths. Your brain interprets them as a stress signal, triggering your body's "fight or flight" reaction. When this protective response is activated, you undergo physiological changes – faster breathing, faster heartbeat, and faster muscle flow – to help you deal with the threat.

Slow, deep breathing, in contrast, counteracts these shifts and encourages relaxation throughout your body and mind by stimulating the body's "rest and digest" functions.

Arianna Huffington[1], founder and CEO of Thrive Global and renowned author, uses the "box" or "square" breathing technique as her go-to method to reduce stress. All you do is inhale for a count

---

1. The "box breathing" technique Arianna Huffington swears by. (2023, May 9). MSNBC.com.
https://www.msnbc.com/know-your-value/health-mindset/box-breathing-technique-arianna-huffington-swears-n1304933

of four, hold for a count of four, and exhale for a count of four. Then, pause and hold for another count of 4. Repeat ten times or until you feel better.

D. Meditate

Meditation means different things depending upon one's culture and beliefs. The definition I use is *to study and consider*. Meditation offers many benefits, such as inner calm, clarity, improved attention, and productivity, by getting you to focus and be present in the moment. You can meditate upon God's creations (Psalm 8), God's wonders (Psalm 77:11), God's word (Psalm 1:2), and God's greatness (Psalm 145:3-7).

E. Rest Your Body

Facing obstacles can prevent you from getting enough sleep. However, obtaining adequate sleep is crucial to your overall health.

I've found that getting enough sleep increases my happiness, focus, productivity, creativity, and overall quality of life. However, when I do not get sufficient rest, I am more likely to feel anxious, irritable, and have a short fuse.

If you have trouble sleeping, try the following:

- Set a sleep and wake-up time for at least seven hours. Then, set reminders and alarms to wind down and wake up.

- Avoid strenuous physical activities that stimulate you at least three hours before night.

- Check that your bed and room temperature are both

comfortable.

- Unwind by doing something calming an hour or two before bedtime.

- Spray your pillow with a scent spray that promotes sleep, like "This Works."

5. Witness the Miracles

There are miracles all around us. Unfortunately, many go unnoticed because we are too preoccupied or take them for granted. Our reasons for doing so may be valid: we are caring for a loved one, worried about our finances, unsure about our health diagnosis, anxious about our job, or something similar.

However, when we are not mindful of the present, we miss the wonder of each moment and do not seize the day.

***

Every day, we have the unique opportunity to
see God's handiwork in action – birds singing,
butterflies fluttering, and rain falling.

***

Even more impressive is that we get another chance to experience our extraordinary lives – our lungs breathing, hearts pumping, eyes blinking, and so much more!

But sadly, we often waste valuable time criticizing, doing things that don't matter, or worrying about tomorrow. Or we deal with theoretical problems in our imaginations that may or may not occur. Can you relate?

Consequently, we miss the "right now" moment. What exactly do I mean? The "right now" moment will not arrive next week. Nor tomorrow. Not even first thing in the morning. But you guessed it; it is right now!

***

> To go through life cavalierly, presuming we will have another precious moment, is like playing Russian roulette with time itself. Time marches on with or without us, so it's wise to slow down and appreciate the beauty of each day.

***

My mother's situation and requirements changed as I cared for her; they could be one way one day and another the next. Despite my need to be in charge, I had to relinquish control. I humbly asked God for provision and grace for that day – for that moment. I couldn't think about 12:01 a.m. because midnight might not come. As a result, I became acutely aware of and appreciated the miracle of each precious moment.

Do you realize you have the gift of being in the present as you read this? This awareness can liberate you from unnecessary concerns, allowing you to experience serenity and joy. Right now.

Will you pause momentarily and whisper thanks for the gift and grace given to you today?

6. Help Others by Planting Seeds

A server approached my table at one of my favorite restaurants, saying, "The couple who sat here paid for your meal, but they want to keep it a secret." I smiled, surprised, because I remembered paying for people's food in drive-through lines for years. I was reaping what I sowed, meaning the positive energies and efforts I put out into the world had returned unexpectedly.

The couple's generosity reminded me of earlier times when someone paid my bill for no reason or extended kindness to me. But those thoughtful deeds did not happen on their own. Instead, they were the fruit of the seeds I'd sown, like money and empathy.

***

When you're going through a terrible time, the last thing on your mind is how to help others. But that is precisely the moment to activate the sowing and reaping principle.

***

Here are a few practical examples:

Emotional Support:
- **Sow**: Offer a listening ear, words of encouragement, or simply your presence to someone going through a tough time.

- **Reap**: In turn, you might find that when you face

challenges, these individuals are there to support you, having been touched by your earlier kindness.

Physical Assistance:
- **Sow**: Help someone with physical tasks they can't manage alone, like moving furniture or fixing a household issue.

- **Reap**: Not only do you build a bond of trust, but you might find others more willing to lend a hand when you need physical help.

Planting seeds during hard times can strengthen bonds, foster community, and create a supportive environment. Plus, it downright feels good! The joy of generosity can't be beat! So, what seeds will you plant today?

7. Remember Your Previous Wins

When we become weighed down by a problem, we lose sight of our capabilities. However, this is an excellent opportunity to reflect on our previous accomplishments because it reveals our character and grit.

Our track record proves that, just as we conquered challenges in the past, we can also overcome this one. And the next.

Take a moment and name a time when you won something. You may have competed in a contest, won a scholarship, or overcome your fear of public speaking. What was it? Remember that feeling. Then, let that achievement encourage you to win again.

8. Have Faith in your Ability to Handle it

As a wedding coordinator decades ago, I ensured the bride had the wedding of her dreams, which was no minor feat. Every detail mattered. For instance, I confirmed that the floral arrangements were on point and that the cake arrived on time and intact. I also verified that the wedding party was ready. Then, with excitement and expectation in the air, the music began, the door opened, and the bride made her grand entrance, much to the delight of the groom and all in attendance. The big day officially began after months of preparation.

To achieve a flawless and memorable event, I coordinated many vendors. I also dealt with various personalities, which required me to use multiple abilities, such as leadership, organization, attention to detail, people skills, resourcefulness, negotiating, and communication.

Guess what? I had no idea I would need these skills in the far future as my mother's caretaker. But instead of vendors, I would arrange medical appointments and transportation. As my mother's advocate, I would battle for her using my leadership, critical thinking, and communication talents.

In retrospect, while I thought I was in the business of making brides happy, perhaps my company was preparing me for something far more significant down the road.

My mother once shared something that sounded nicer than any music I'd heard at the weddings I planned. She said that parents worry about their children's futures and how they will navigate life

– that she knew my brother and I was smart, but seeing me handle everything for her made her proud because I was such a natural.

I accepted her praise, smiling, and said, *"Mom, I was born for this."*

It's natural to feel overwhelmed and inadequate when confronted with a new challenge. But while you may believe that you are over your head and that the task is too difficult, consider this: You are "built" and "equipped" for your situation. You have everything you need to get through it. I believe in you. Do you?

***

As unbelievable as it may seem, you have been preparing for such a time as this.

***

9. Dress Up

As I walked to my car at a shopping outlet, a stranger said, *"You look like Beyoncé! You belong in Hollywood! What are you doing here?"* She stopped me, saying she saw me from afar, admired my outfit, and had an aura about me. Her name was Suzanne.

Smiling and thanking her, I told Suzanne that her compliments meant a lot to me, especially since I had been going through an ordeal but wanted to look nice despite my circumstances.

Suzanne didn't know I'd planned to dress casually in jeans and a blouse. But a friend of mine, Roslyn, encouraged me to put on something cute.

So I took her suggestion. Looking in my closet, I found the cute, chic two-piece outfit from Saks Fifth Avenue I'd not worn. It was the kind you might wear to a beach resort. The top cropped at my waist, and the lace pants flared out. I wore my hair up, applied minimal makeup, and topped it off with the perfect earrings.

I felt like royalty! I even walked like a queen! Strutted is a better word! With my head up and shoulders back, I commanded the walkway as if it were my runway! Although I received many compliments that day, I was not seeking attention; I just wanted to feel confident like my old self.

So, dress up when you're feeling down! Wear whatever makes you happy on the inside. It does not have to be elaborate or expensive. Simply dress like you're blessed, not going through a test! Your light might attract others to you. Who knows? People could see God's glory even if they don't know your story!

By the way, Suzanne and I've become acquaintances who occasionally meet for lunch, listening to one another or laughing so hard we come close to crying!

10. Smile Through Your Trial

Let's be honest. It can be difficult to tackle challenges with a smile on your face. How can you keep a positive attitude while your world crumbles? How do you keep smiling in light of abuse or a devastating diagnosis? It's not easy. But your smile is like a superpower. Here's how it works:

- A smile instills optimism in the air.

- A smile conveys happiness, calls for peace, and inspires

hope.

- A smile draws positive energy like a magnet.

- A smile causes others to smile back.

Here's an illustration. I'm usually a happy person who smiles when I greet someone. So, while waiting in line at an airport, I smiled at a lady, who smiled back. Shortly afterward, I felt a tap on my shoulder. I couldn't imagine who it was or what they wanted. When I turned around, to my surprise, a woman said, *"Thank you for that smile."* She was the same woman I casually greeted moments before! I responded, *"You're welcome,"* beaming inside. I wondered if she was going through anything. Was she sad? Lonely? Or did she simply appreciate that a stranger at a busy and crowded airport made eye contact and acknowledged her?

I'll never find out the answer. Yet I know that a simple act of kindness drew together two strangers. And everything else seemed trivial.

11. Be Kind to Yourself

I stayed with my mother in a different city from where I lived throughout her illness. After a time, I returned home for some much-needed rest. My absence became obvious.

To my dismay, I noticed piles of documents in my office, a clear reminder of unfinished business. The clothes hamper overflowed. In my living room, dust balls danced across the floor.

If you're anything like me, you prefer everything to be in order. Then "life happens," and your plans go out the window. Your schedule changes, your "to-do" list needs to get done, and you cannot meet the high standard you have set for yourself.

As a result, pressure rises like a kettle of boiling water. What are you going to do?

When you're going through a difficult situation, it can be downright impossible to do "all the things." While you have good intentions, time and energy are not on your side. You don't have time to return a phone call or text message. Or you want to avoid talking to anyone because you're exhausted from getting through the day or deciding what to do next.

Here are four words to free you from being too hard on yourself: *"It's okay as is."* Say them out loud and let them resonate.

Remember, no one is perfect. You are not a superhero. As a result, snatch the "S" from your chest. Replace any feelings of self-doubt and self-pity with self-compassion and love.

***

> Refuse to fall into the painful trap of guilt. Instead,
> make your way to the magnificent throne of grace.

***

I invite you to extend grace to yourself. To put it another way, be kind to yourself. Forgive and love yourself more than ever, and move on without stress or unrealistic expectations.

When you do this, you honor yourself and express gratitude for *who* you are *as* you are.

So, inhale deeply. Exhale slowly and repeat these words: *"It's okay as is."*

12. Recognize When to Let Go

Problems, as you know, can weigh you down like a ton of bricks. You may feel like you can't come up for air, and the weight of it will crush you.

Nonetheless, you must address the problem because it's not going away. But how? My cousin, Kay, who has been through her share of adversities, once told me, *"When you're face-to-face with hard times, you do what you must to get through it without giving it much thought."*

You must "soldier on" even if you don't know your next move. Even if you don't have the strength to take another step. So, before you find yourself empty and exhausted, unable to help anyone else, I encourage you to let go.

***

I'm not saying give in. Instead, relax your grip and surrender your situation to God. I understand how difficult this is. However, I discovered that when you release it *to* Him, you rely *on* Him and can then rest *in* Him.

***

It's also worth emphasizing that removing your hands from the situation does not imply that you don't care about it. However, it shows you are wise enough to entrust God with your battle. And He is fully willing and capable of achieving victory on your behalf!

I eventually let go of trying to control the tsunami of events about my mother's care by handing them to God and entirely trusting Him. When I got out of my way, I saw God show up mightily.

Remember, we can get to calmer waters using the proper tools.

Which one of these strategies speaks to you the most?

Chapter 4

Pressing Forward

"The great courageous act that we must all do is to have the courage to step out of our history and past so we can live our dreams."
~Oprah Winfrey

If you're dealing with disappointments, failures, or other emotional stress, you may feel like you can't do this right now. Regardless of the source, these raw and real feelings can affect your daily life. Here's my advice to you:

***

Don't despair; your newfound happiness is just
beyond the shadows of your heartache.

***

Please understand that you cannot experience joy with your head bowed and shoulders bent toward the ground. It's just not happening. Instead, straighten your back, stand tall, and raise your head as though reaching towards the heavens! Allow God to give you the serenity He wants for you. That's correct. The Almighty desires that "little old you" experience His calm that exceeds comprehension, and only He can provide it (Philippians 4: 6-7). So take a stand, decide to receive that peace, and make your anguish and anxiety ineffective! Hear me. Now is the time to fight – for your future, family, finances, and faith!

But you may think, *Rhonda, how do I fight when I don't have the strength to function? Where do I go for solace when I'm alone at night? To whom do I turn when no one seems to hear my desperate cries?*

Although there's no "one size fits all" solution to move from sadness to serenity, it begins with changing our mindset. We must decide not to remain in the same situation. We can start by adopting this simple mantra during our struggles: Keep going despite the challenges.

***

Pressing forward entails more than just moving forward. Instead, it involves actively pushing against the opposition that impedes your progress and using force to achieve your goal.
***

Here are several strategies with examples for advancing.

1. Choose to Move

Even if you have excellent intentions, you must act.

God's grace empowers us with the intrinsic ability to choose how we respond to adversity, whether the situation resulted from our choices or events beyond our control.

So, when misfortune hits you, you must make some choices. You can continue to have a daily pity party that sucks the life out of you. Alternatively, you can go through the motions of each day, feeling unmotivated. Or you can strive for a more meaningful existence that makes you happy when you get out of bed each morning.

You say, *Rhonda, I don't feel like smiling, getting out of bed, or even facing the day.* I've been there and done that. It's perfectly fine if that's how you feel. You're not in a race, so go at your own pace. But try to do one thing that will get you closer to moving on with your life.

God desires for you to have abundant peace and happiness. But you must take the steps. In other words, you must start going even if you don't know where or how you will get there. We've established that staying stuck and stationary isn't a choice. No way.

***

Moving closer to your future requires making a determined decision – then action – sometimes every day, sometimes every hour.

***

If this is scary, just "jump and grow wings on the way down."

Dr. Martin Luther King Jr., a prominent Civil Rights Leader from the United States during the Jim Crow Era in America, once said to his followers, *"If you can't fly, then run; if you can't run, then walk; if you can't walk, then crawl, but whatever you do, you have to keep moving forward."*

King's eloquent statement from decades ago still applies today. So, commit to doing whatever it takes to get started, and then do it without hesitation.

Some practical things you may do to start moving are:

<u>A. Change Your Routines</u>

If you're feeling low because of losing a loved one, gaining a few more pounds, or anything else that creates stress, it's easy to find yourself in a rut. However, you don't have to stay there.

A small change in your daily routine might break the cycle of negative emotions, provide a fresh perspective, and promote a sense of accomplishment. Furthermore, switching your schedule requires little work. To keep it simple, don't overthink it and suffer from analysis paralysis. Trying anything new is easy if you take bold baby steps.

Changing your routine during challenging times can offer numerous benefits. Here's a list of these advantages, with examples:

1. <u>*Breaks Monotony*</u>:

    Benefit: A change in routine can provide a fresh perspective and break the cycle of repetitive thoughts or behaviors. *Example: If you're in a rut with a work project, changing your work environment, like working from a coffee shop or a park, can stimulate creativity.*

2. <u>Reduces Stress</u>:
Benefit: New activities or a different routine can act as a distraction, giving your mind a break from stressors. *Example: If you're grieving, taking up a new hobby like painting or gardening can offer moments of relief and focus.*

3. <u>Boosts Mental Flexibility</u>:
Benefit: Adapting to a new routine can stretch you mentally, allowing you to adapt to future changes. *Example: If you've lost a job, adjusting your daily routine to include skill-building or networking can improve your prospects and make you more adaptable to different roles.*

4. <u>Encourages Personal Growth</u>:
Benefit: Facing and adapting to changes can lead to personal development and discovering strengths you didn't know you had. *Example: If you're going through a breakup, joining a support group or reading self-help books can lead to personal insights and growth.*

5. <u>Provides a Sense of Control:</u>
Benefit: When external circumstances are challenging, changing your routine can give you control over your life. *Example: During a health crisis, creating a new fitness or*

dietary program can give you a feeling of taking proactive steps towards recovery.

6. <u>Enhances Physical Health:</u>
Benefit: A new routine can encourage physical activity or better habits, improving health. *Example: If you're depressed, incorporating daily walks or yoga can boost endorphins and improve mood.*

7. <u>Opportunity for New Social Connections:</u>
Benefit: Trying out new activities or routines can lead to meeting new people and forming supportive relationships. *Example: If you've moved to a new city and feel lonely, joining a club or group activity can help you make new friends.*

8. <u>Breaks Negative Patterns:</u>
Benefit: Changing your routine can disrupt negative habits or thought patterns, paving the way for positive behaviors. *Example: If you're struggling with addiction, altering your routine to avoid triggers and include supportive activities can be crucial for recovery.*

9. <u>Boosts Productivity:</u>
Benefit: A fresh routine can increase efficiency and motivation. *Example: If you're experiencing burnout, changing your work hours or incorporating more breaks can rejuvenate your productivity.*

10. *Encourages Mindfulness and Presence:*
    Benefit: New routines or activities require more conscious thought, promoting mindfulness. *Example: If you're feeling disconnected, adopting a daily meditation or journaling practice can foster a deeper connection with your thoughts and feelings.*

B. Take a Mental Break

Everyone can experience brain overload. It's easy to become overwhelmed by racing thoughts or unfinished responsibilities. Taking a mental break to slow down can refresh and rejuvenate you.

Your downtime can range from ten minutes to several hours. What you do differs depending on what makes sense to you. Choose something that will divert your attention away from consuming thoughts. Consider the following activities for your mental break:

- Have lunch away from the office (one of my favorites).

- Watch an entertaining television show or listen to soothing jazz music.

- Talk to a friend.

- Play card games on your computer.

- Unplug from social media.

What will your mental break look like?

C. Spend Time Alone with God

It's easy to become self-reliant in our do-it-yourself era, feeling that we can do practically anything with our strength and ability. For example, we can search YouTube, Google, or Artificial Intelligence (AI) for training or information.

***

> Coaches offer perspectives, programs, podcasts, and pep talks to help us through our challenges. While beneficial, even the best self-help gurus and books can only help to a limited extent.

***

Some problems will inevitably require the intervention of a higher power. Connecting (or reconnecting) with God may be prudent during these moments. After all, who better to converse with than God?

Your alone time with God is personal; how you spend time in His presence differs from how someone else does. You could, for example, pray to God. You might even pray at a specific time or throughout the day. Don't worry if you don't know what to say. Talk to Him openly. Thank God for what He has done, and ask Him what He wants to do *for* you and *through* you. Remember that this is a two-way street, so pay attention to His response as He reveals Himself to you through His Word.

Another method you might connect with God is through praise. Psalm 22:3 says, *"God inhabits the praises of His people."*

Honoring and exalting God is what it means to glorify Him. So declare His goodness even when faced with affliction, knowing God is present.

D. Spend Time Alone With Yourself

When stressed or frustrated, some push themselves to work harder and become consumed by performing tasks.

While distracting ourselves from our predicament to numb our feelings or ignore the issue may help, it is usually only a temporary solution. Disregarding or burying your sentiments by working harder merely delays the inevitable – sooner or later, you must face and deal with your problem.

Instead of becoming a busy bee, prioritize meaningful time for yourself. Here are several suggestions to get you started.

- Go for a walk, swing, or shoot hoops in a park.

- Sit in your car or take a drive.

- Soak in the bathtub or enjoy a relaxing shower.

- Play music or listen to an audiobook.

- Journal, color, write, craft, or paint.

- Meditate on God's wonders and His word.

- Find an app that helps you relax.

E. Allow for Imperfections

Everyone has flaws. That means you and me. You will undoubtedly say and do things while dealing with adversity or pain you wish to take back or redo. But words stick, and you can't take them back. Similarly, time passes, and you cannot retrieve it. However, there's good news!

***

God loves you regardless of what others think of you
or what you believe of yourself.

***

Therefore, allow imperfections to mold you into a better version of yourself – a better daughter or son, sibling, spouse, friend, neighbor, or coworker.

Accepting your flaws has an array of positive consequences. Here are several benefits:

- It opens the doors to personal growth and development.

- It allows you to be authentic and genuine.

- It reduces the pressures of unrealistic expectations.

- It enriches your connections with others.

- It makes you more empathetic and compassionate.

- It cultivates resilience and adaptability.

- It promotes emotional well-being.

F. Practice Forgiving Others

Resentment is a natural reaction when someone causes you pain, offends you, or does not do something they promised. However, if we want to increase our well-being, we must forgive.

According to The Grief Recovery Institute's founders and writers of "The Grief Recovery Handbook," John W. James and Russell Friedman, *"Any memorized resentment of past events will limit and restrict our ability to participate fully in life. Any reminder of the person or situation may cause a painful revisiting of the unfinished feelings associated with it."*[1]

Did you know that we do not have to tell someone we forgive them, especially if they have not asked for it? According to the authors, *"You can quietly absolve them by identifying what they did or did not do that hurt you and declaring that you will not allow them to hurt you again."* Taking this position enables you to reclaim your power and go forward.

G. Motivate Yourself

You will feel discouraged at times, regardless of your position in life. And, like most others, when discouragement strikes, you turn to a genuine friend or a trusted family member for support. But how can you keep going when no one appears to have the right words to soothe your soul? What if you need someone to show up

---

1. James, & Friedman. (n.d.). The Grief Recovery Handbook.

for you and they don't? Do you give up, or do you dig within? You encourage yourself.

"When nobody else celebrates you, learn to celebrate yourself," Joel Osteen, an American pastor, televangelist, and author, once told his audience. *"When nobody else compliments you, then compliment yourself. It's not up to other people to keep you encouraged; it's up to you. Encouragement should come from inside."*

This quote sounds terrific, but how do you go about doing it? Here are several ways to cheer yourself up:

- Keep God's promises in mind.

- Read encouraging words.

- Concentrate your efforts on inspiring others.

- Make a list of positive affirmations about yourself.

- Compliment yourself.

- Turn your disappointment into the drive to succeed.

- Look at how far you've come.

2. Feel Free to Express Yourself

I began to cry while visiting a church in Rwanda, Africa, standing on the stage to speak. Overcome with emotion, the tears flowed because I felt I'd come home. Afterward, a young lady came to me, saying my vulnerability drew her to me because Rwandans are taught not to cry. I smiled and hugged her, thankful several counselors encouraged me to do just that. They told me, *"Expressing your emotions is good for you."* From my experience, I believe it's healthy and helpful to "feel your feels!" This individual benefited from me doing just that.

For example, when my mother went to hospice and the truth of her condition became clear, I let my tears fall like rain, releasing months of pent-up sorrow.

After about ten minutes of crying, admitting the agony, and accepting my helplessness, I felt a "painful peace." Though the doctor's prognosis broke my heart, I was happy that Mom would receive the care she needed and deserved.

When forced to confront a challenging situation, you may experience many emotions – despair, anger, anxiety, confusion, empathy, fear, sadness, and guilt. Do any of these resonate?

If so, remember that it is typical for you to resist these feelings by keeping them inside and avoiding them. However, feeling these emotions is normal if you have experienced a challenging situation. While it may not feel pleasant, embracing your feelings helps you heal. Here's the deal: If you can name your emotions, you can manage them and move on.

But what happens when you have a flood of emotions? Express them, but don't stress or obsess over them. For example, during difficult times, I've been at the extreme ends of the emotion spectrum. I felt exhausted and elated on some days and overwhelmed and honored on others. And it was okay.

Similarly, you may experience excitement one minute and emptiness the next. The important thing is to allow yourself to feel so you can heal.

Contact a qualified therapist or trusted pastor if you need help handling your emotions.

3. Set up a Support System

A robust support system is necessary to help you stay the course during difficult times.

As I previously said, my spouse, Doug, supported me when my mom became ill. For example, he prayed for me and asked others to do the same. He also often inquired as to how I was doing. And I felt relieved when he traveled up and down the road to be with me. Doug helped me in far too many ways to count, and I cannot thank him enough.

My family, friends, grief support groups, and strangers showed they cared differently. Some ran errands, answered phone calls, sent thank you cards, and prepared meals. Others quietly sat with me and listened. And still others, like my good friend Norma, prayed for me daily.

People who support you are a source of strength and inspiration because they uplift you with thoughtful gestures. Knowing they're thinking about you and cheering for you gives you the nudge to keep going.

So, make it a point to establish friendships now. Genuinely connect with others and be there for them. Then, when the tables turn, they are more likely to be there for you.

4. Practice Gratitude

Feeling thankful during difficult circumstances can sometimes seem paradoxical. Let's face it. When consumed with problems, we tend to overlook how fortunate we are. Yet, practicing gratitude during chaos, crises, and confusion can be a powerful way to shift your perspective and foster resilience. Here are several ways to practice gratitude, along with clear and simple steps:

A. Gratitude Journaling:

Step 1: Every day, set aside 5-10 minutes.

Step 2: Write down three things you're grateful for, big or small.

Step 3: Reflect on why you're thankful for each item.

B. Gratitude Jar:

Step 1: Find a jar and some small pieces of paper.

Step 2: Every day, write one thing you're grateful for on paper.

Step 3: Place it in the jar to positively reflect on over time.

C. Gratitude Walks:

Step 1: Take a 10-20 minute walk outside.

Step 2: As you walk, notice the sky, trees, or buildings.

Step 3: Reflect on what you're grateful for during your walk.

D. Gratitude Meditation:

Step 1: Find a quiet space and sit comfortably.

Step 2: Close your eyes and take a few deep breaths.

Step 3: Reflect on a person or thing you're grateful for.

E. Gratitude Letters:
Step 1: Think of someone who's positively impacted your life.
Step 2: Write them a letter expressing your gratitude.
Step 3: If you feel comfortable, send the letter. Or keep it.

F. Mindful Moments:
Step 1: Pause a few times throughout your day.
Step 2: Find one thing you're grateful for in that moment.
Step 3: Acknowledge this gratitude internally or jot it down.

G. Gratitude Reminders:
Step 1: Set reminders on your phone to pause and reflect.
Step 2: When the reminder goes off, stop what you're doing.
Step 3: Think of one thing you're grateful for.

H. Gratitude Conversations:
Step 1: Find someone to share with.
Step 2: Take turns discussing things you're grateful for.
Step 3: Listen actively and validate each other's feelings.

In the face of adversity, taking the first steps to move forward is essential. Expressing our feelings, surrounding ourselves with a supportive community, and practicing gratitude can illuminate the silver linings, guiding us toward brighter days.

CHAPTER 5

Turning Your Pain into Gain

"New beginnings are often disguised as painful endings." ~Lao Tzu

Picture the following scenarios. You signed the last page of your divorce papers, your mortgage lender sent you a final foreclosure notice, and your boss informed you that you are no longer needed. But there's more.

Your child has landed herself in trouble again. Your friend also got horrible news concerning their medical report, and you lost a close family member. While not all these problems will coincide, even one could rock your world. When it does, the question becomes, *What now?*

I can confirm from personal experience that the pain of such situations can leave you feeling devastated. For example, my mother's unexpected illness and death left me in a state of shock, numb from head to toe. But guess what? I made it. And I'm still here! On two legs! On firm ground! Please say the following three words: *"I'm still standing."* Were there days when I wanted to throw in the towel? Heck, yes! However, I made a different choice.

***

I decided to turn my sorrow into a solution.

***

In doing so, I found no fast track to dealing with your pain. You must work to cope if your hurt arises from grief, uncertainty, rejection, loneliness, or something else. However, you can benefit from your suffering with time, commitment, and a plan. After all, you owe it to the Lord, yourself, your family, and even strangers who need to hear your story. So, don't let your past hurt delay your future promise. Instead, learn from your experience.

According to Psychologist Richard G. Tedeschi's "Growth After Trauma" essay in the Harvard Business Review, *"Post-traumatic growth is the good that arises from a difficult life experience."*[1]

And, yes, growth and good can come. For example, my adversity has enabled me to:

1. Value the Little Things in Life

I've learned to slow down and appreciate life's simple things, which I took for granted. Enjoying these treasures anchors me in

---

1. Growth After Trauma. (2020, July 1). Harvard Business Review. https://hbr.org/2020/07/growth-after-trauma

the present, grounding me. It lets me get the most out of each day and lowers my stress.

Every morning, for example, I thank God for another day. Hearing the birds chirp and seeing the deer run across my yard delights me. I enjoy having the financial means to eat out at a restaurant. And mingling with family and friends revitalizes my Spirit. The list of little things I've come to appreciate isn't so little. It's infinite. I've also found that ordinary things will bring you enormous fulfillment.

Here are eight ideas to get you thinking.
- Get up early and embrace the day,
- Each day, concentrate on the good.
- Surround yourself with positive people.
- Keep a notebook of the kind things others do for you.
- Every day, say something encouraging to someone.
- When possible, go out of your way to help others.
- Laugh often.
- Smile when greeting others.

2. Show Sympathy Towards Others

Empathizing with others means feeling their suffering, stress, and frustrations. Spending countless sleepless hours caring for my mom has made me more sensitive to others in need – from a homeless person begging for money to a single mother struggling to connect with her child. They both have urgent needs. And if the Spirit leads me to help them, I will do anything I can.

Some people believe they have nothing to contribute if they do not give money. Yet, money is only one solution to some of the world's many problems today.

***

> Compassion for others doesn't require an abundance of wealth. However, it takes a grateful heart and a strong desire to touch the lives of others positively.

***

Everyone innately can show compassion to someone in need, no matter how small it may appear. For instance, you can actively listen, offer emotional support or resources, and accept them without judgment.

Being compassionate has had significant positive impacts on my life. Here are a few:

- Helping others gives me a sense of purpose.

- My relationships with family and friends have strengthened.

- I have less stress and anxiety.

- I have grown personally and enjoy life more.

- I am more resilient because I receive compassion.

3. Encourage Others in Their Difficult Moments

Who doesn't need a little pep talk now and then? If you answered no one, you're right!

Because you're human, your heart will ache sooner or later due to a traumatic experience in your own life, the lives of those you care about, or even strangers.

And when that happens, encouraging words can often help you get through the day. It makes no difference if they are from a family member or a stranger.

I can count the times a three-minute phone call, card, text, visit, or hug restored my Spirit for the day. Those small actions were a beacon of brightness amidst those dark times.

And because of the kindness of others, I feel obliged to go the extra mile to make someone else's day brighter. As mentioned in an earlier chapter, I regard it as seed sowing. According to the scriptures, people reap what they sow (Galatians 6:7-9). So, I've decided to plant seeds of encouragement in the lives of people who need it.

It doesn't matter if it's a teen who failed their driver's exam or someone who lost everything in a storm.

You can also find a place in your heart and time in your day to support others going through difficult times. Who knows? You could have the answer or inspiration they're looking for.

Here are eight positive actions that will brighten someone's day:

- Let them know you're thinking about them.

- Tell them, *"I'm here for you."* And be present.

- If they need prayer, ask if you may pray for them.

- When you see them, smile and call their name.

- Call them to say hello instead of texting.

- Offer to go grocery shopping for them.

- Send them a gift card.

- Offer to run errands.

4. Develop Your Resilience

Resilience refers to the ability of an individual to adapt well and recover quickly after facing adversity, trauma, tragedy, threats, or significant sources of stress. It embodies the capacity to bounce back and maintain or regain one's emotional balance.

Resilience today, tomorrow, and forever is one of my slogans. Although my mother died from sickness, she battled bravely till the end. And her strong will has left an indelible imprint on me, refining my concept of resilience. As a result, I now understand the saying, "What doesn't kill you makes you stronger." When I make a personal goal, I don't let anything stand in my way; if necessary, I'll go through or around any hurdles. I may wince in agony when I meet a stumbling block, but I will bounce back, dig in my heels, and continue until I break through.

And know what? You, too, can turn your adversity into an advantage.

Will it be difficult? Will you have to overcome considerable obstacles? Will you have any doubts now and then? Yes, to all these concerns. But don't worry; if you're resilient, you'll succeed. Here's how:

- Use your discomfort as a teaching opportunity.

- Accept your pain and remind yourself of its rewards.

- Allow your sorrow to bring forth the best in you.

- Use your pain as motivation to achieve greater heights.

- Set high standards for yourself.

- Tell your story to motivate others to achieve their goals.

- Remove the word "failure" from your vocabulary.

- Maintain your focus and discipline.

- Look for the bright side.

5. Increase Your Self-esteem

Tragedies are excruciatingly painful. They can knock the wind out of your sails, leaving you feeling defeated. Heartbreaks might make you question if you have what it takes to go forward, let alone live a productive life. My mother's demise left me feeling dejected and overwhelmed with despair.

Nonetheless, I realized I had to learn to benefit from my terrible grief. I didn't want my mother's passing to be in vain. But I must admit that there were times when I wondered if I could do it. How would I go about it? Then, when I was deep in my dismal debate, the lights came on.

***

I brushed off the dust, recognizing that the worst-case scenario had already occurred. And the world hadn't ended yet.

***

By God's grace, I survived. I got knocked down but not knocked out! That's correct. I got my mojo back. And I restored my self-esteem, believing I could do anything if I could only get through this painful ordeal! Large or small challenges would pale compared to the ones I overcame

Here's what happened next. I started proclaiming victory and achievement over my life instead of succumbing to self-defeat. I made a list of positive affirmations about myself to inspire me to reach for the stars in anything I set my mind to do. I gave my situation to God to use for my good. But not only for my benefit but also for the good of others I meet.

I challenge you to use your trials as a catalyst to increase your self-esteem, just like I did. Begin by writing down and repeating positive self-affirmations throughout the day. Here are several examples to get you started:

- *"I am a survivor and thriver."*
- *"I can overcome any obstacle."*
- *"I am brilliant."*
- *"I dedicate myself to inspiring people."*
- *"I only expect the best from myself."*
- *"I will not give up until I reach the finish line."*
- *"I bring out the best in people."*
- *"I will learn how to move forward and upward."*
- *"I will fulfill my purpose on this planet."*

Next, turn your words into action.

6. Place Your faith in God

Nothing brings you closer to God than a bit of adversity in your life, whether from situations within or outside your control. When heartache hits you, what do you do? When the pain becomes debilitating, to whom do you turn?

There is no single solution to cope with pain.

Thankfully, I've always had faith in the Lord. Yet, staying by my mother's side till she breathed her last breath elevated my faith in the Lord to a higher level. She often asked my husband and me to pray for her, which we were honored to do.

Despite her dire circumstances, she kept her faith in the Lord. Seeing my mother's unshakeable faith in God confirmed that God's Word is true. "*He is the same yesterday, today, and forever*" *(Hebrews 13:8).*

I often saw God's intervention in my life, both during and after my mother's illness. And today, more than ever, I'm confident that God can "*... do exceedingly abundantly above all that we ask or think (Ephesians 3:20).*

I'm glad to say that my mother's passing, albeit devastating for me because I loved her so much, has caused me to trust God more. I didn't realize it initially, but I thank God daily for turning my pain into a gain. As a result, I've grown to trust that:

- God will bring me comfort through difficult times.

- God will supply my needs at the proper time.

- God will help me learn and grow. n

- God will help my heart to remain pure.

- God will hear my pleading and come to my aid.

- God will order my steps to walk out His will.

So, what is my bottom-line message to you? It's straightforward:

***

Accept your pain, even if it is excruciating.

***

Allow God to shape your character and change you into the best version of yourself by using your tears, setbacks, disappointments, and any other unpleasant emotions you may experience. Of course, going from a painful situation to a purpose-driven life requires courage. Still, take heart, knowing that *"in all things God works for the good of those who love Him..." (Romans 8:28).*

Also, remember in every shadow of pain lies the potential for growth and transformation. Embrace life's challenges as catalysts, turning setbacks into success stories. With resilience and perspective, what is once hurt can become the very force that propels you forward, turning pain into unparalleled gain!

Chapter 6

Reaching Your Destiny

"You can accomplish far greater things when you depend on a higher power." ~Lailah Gifty Akita

You endured many sleepless nights and overcame challenges that most people cannot fathom. Still, by God's grace and goodness, you survived. Will you pause right now and say thanks? You can now see the light at the end of the tunnel, which motivates you to stay on the course. You see, smell, and taste your destiny even though you have yet to arrive. You feel something incredible awaits you. You're sure that God didn't allow you to endure life's storms to live a life of mediocrity. So, get to it! Now! Destiny's calling your name!

But how do you respond?

First, let's discuss destiny since it's often confused with fate. You see, your life choices determine your destiny, which you have control over. However, fate refers to events in your life that are beyond your control – in other words, fate is the hand that God dealt you. For example, you're running late for your dream job interview, and the rush hour traffic has come to a standstill because of a ten-car crash, which causes you to miss your interview.

On the other hand, let's say Linda has a speech impediment. Yet, she still aspires to someday grace the "big stage" as a renowned motivational speaker. So, as a child, she constantly asked her parents to get her a private speech therapist to boost her self-confidence. To her delight, they do. As an adolescent, Linda continued developing her speaking abilities by joining Toastmasters and online support groups, getting a mentor, and accepting every opportunity to speak before a live audience despite shaking in her boots from anxiety and still stuttering.

Finally, Linda obtained her Bachelor's, Master's, and Doctorate degrees in Speech-Language Pathology. As a mature adult, Linda speaks to standing-room-only crowds, leaving them in awe because of her articulate and elegant speech delivery. Well, it's safe to say that our imaginary role model, Linda, reached her destiny. Guess what? So can you, with the right strategies.

***

> It doesn't matter if you grew up in a single-parent, dysfunctional, or impoverished household. Or even if you've suffered several disasters and setbacks beyond your control. You can still reach your destiny.

***

But here's the deal: There are no shortcuts. The pathway is demanding and requires your absolute best effort, but so does running a 26-mile marathon, working two jobs as a single parent, losing 50 pounds of stubborn fat, quitting bad habits, or achieving any other great accomplishment.

So put on your game face and shake off whatever dead weight impedes you. It's time to make it happen! Your destiny is not to be delayed or denied! Former First Lady Eleanor Roosevelt said, *"The future belongs to those who believe in the beauty of their dreams."*

Here's the roadmap to reach your destiny:

1. Decide What You Want Out of Life

<u>*A. Seek God's Guidance*</u>

When contemplating your destiny, you should always seek the counsel of the Almighty Himself to guide you in the right direction and order your steps. God gave us distinct abilities and gifts to live meaningfully and purposefully.

We communicate with God through prayer, which might be a sincere request for help. God will respond to your request for wisdom or direction through His written Word. So, start your day with a dialogue with the Lord to create the positive energy and peaceful atmosphere needed to help you make sound decisions.

<u>*B. Identify Your Aspirations*</u>

Identifying your aspirations involves reflecting on your passions, interests, values, and long-term goals. Begin by answering these questions:

- What makes you feel fulfilled and sets you on fire?

- Where do you envision yourself in the future?

- What are your natural gifts?

- What is your zone of genius?

- What do you want your legacy to be?

Journaling or taking an online assessment might prove insightful if you're unsure. Even family and friends could offer clarity.

If you feel like you're heading in the wrong direction, don't despair. Instead, listen to your heart and trust your instincts. According to Wellness in Real Life creator Dr. Tasha Holland-Kornegay, *"Our brains always use logic and emotions to come to conclusions. We all strive to make the smartest decision in any given circumstance."* She continues, *"And sometimes trusting our gut feeling is the best way to do that."*[1]

2. Set Clear Goals

Goals are crucial in reaching our destiny by providing direction and focus. Once you've identified your passion, set SMART goals – Specific, Measurable, Actionable, Realistic, and Timely. We

---

1. https://www.fastcompany.com/90526352/5-ways-to-get-better-at-trusting-your-gut (Tasha and Hock)

increase our chances of reaching our intended destiny by aligning our ambitions with our aspirations.

3. Create an Action Plan

Each of your specific goals requires a well-thought-out action plan. Otherwise, they're just fantasies. Break down your larger goals into manageable tasks and start working on them. Your action plan should include a schedule for completing each activity, which helps you hold yourself accountable.

4. Reassess Your Strategy

It's a good idea to rethink your strategy periodically. Because circumstances can change beyond your control, plan to adapt as needed. Some adjustments require more work than others. Still, stay focused on the big picture and keep moving forward.

5. Find a Mentor

Don't hesitate to seek support from mentors, peers, or professionals. They can provide valuable advice, guidance, and encouragement. As an award-winning mentor, I've enjoyed seeing the women I've counseled overcome setbacks and flourish beyond their wildest dreams.

Angela Blount, a well-known author, once said in *Once Upon an Ever After*, "Sometimes the most scenic roads in life are the detours you didn't mean to take." I can relate to this as a late bloomer myself. However, a great mentor can help you stay on the fast track to your destiny – helping you avoid landmines, shining objects, and rabbit holes that often hinder your progression.

Mentors come in many forms: coworkers, teachers, family members, friends, subject matter experts, or anyone you believe qualified to help you reach your goal. So, do your homework and choose someone fit for you – someone qualified and with your best interests at heart.

Consider the following about mentors:

A Mentor Understands Your Ultimate Goal

Your mentor must understand where you are coming from and where you want to go. If the blind lead the blind, both will fall into the ditch. So, make sure your mentor clarifies their understanding of your goals.

A Mentor Excels in their Field

Your mentor should know a great deal about the subject you need help navigating; their knowledge and understanding must exceed yours. If not, you're depriving yourself of a straight pathway to your destiny. Your mentor must also be competent to keep you on track to succeed.

A Mentor Provides Candid Feedback

It is in your best interest to build trust and establish a clear line of communication with your mentor. It helps you, in the long run, to get honest feedback about your progression. The truth stings sometimes, but it is needed to stay the course. So, if you ever suspect your mentor isn't giving it to you straight, don't be afraid to speak up. This journey is yours. Consequently, it's up to you to figure out where you stand and how to continue.

6. Expect to be Successful

People define success differently. Everyone must define success for themselves and then make it a reality. Denis Waitley, an American best-selling author and International Speakers' Hall of Fame inductee, equated success to victory. *"All winners, no matter what their game, start with the expectation that they will succeed. Winners say, 'I want to do this, and I CAN do this, not 'I would like to do this, but I don't think I can.'"*

***

Your mindset, more than anything else, determines whether you succeed.

***

7. Stay Even-Keeled

What does it mean to be even-keeled?

It's an expression that describes a person's ability to remain level-headed in all situations, both good and bad.

You will inevitably face hurdles along the way to your destiny. Still, as the saying goes, "Things are never as bad as they appear." Likewise, things are never as good as they appear. So, regardless of what's happening around you, stay focused on your purpose without riding an emotional roller coaster of highs and lows.

8. Get Back on Your Feet After a Fall

Condition yourself to overcome unexpected punches. So when life's events knock you down, hop back on your feet! After all, a heavyweight fighter does not lose a match when knocked down.

Instead, they lose because they fail to get back up. So don't stay down; get up! To reach your destiny, you must have the mindset of a champion – staying on the mat is not an option!

"...When you fail at something, it's not a sign that you're incapable," an unnamed boxing trainer once said. *"Instead, it's a test to determine if you're willing to work even harder to do what you've been doing up to this point – but times ten."*

9. Learn and Grow

Accept that making mistakes is part of the journey. Use these as learning opportunities. For instance, if your first city-wide cleanup has a low turnout, seek feedback and learn what you could improve for better engagement next time.

10. Surround Yourself with Good Vibes

Energy, positive and negative, is contagious. No "Debbie Downers" or "Negative Nancies" allowed! Associate with people with positive energy and a high vibe – that lifts you! These people create an atmosphere to excel. Operating in this environment makes you feel calm, hopeful, and enthusiastic about your circumstances and future.

11. Assist Others

People notice when you go out of your way to help others reach their goals. This gesture encourages them to look for opportunities to return the favor. Assisting others in need makes you feel good about yourself and serves as a role model for those watching.

I still live by the ancient proverb, "What goes around comes around." Therefore, activate your blessings by offering your fellow sisters and brothers a hand up.

To sum it up, embrace your journey to destiny by envisioning your desired destination based on your passion. Set clear goals and chart your course with actionable plans. Seek guidance from mentors, and always anticipate success. Despite the hurdles, persevere with unwavering determination, and let upbeat energy guide you.

My friends, destiny is calling. What will you do today to answer the call?

Chapter 7

Empowering Lives

"A hero is someone who, in spite of weakness, doubt, or not always knowing the answers, goes ahead and overcomes anyway."
~Christopher Reeve

Heroes exist everywhere. Don't believe me? Just look around your community, house, or even the mirror.

In previous chapters, I gave inspiration and action steps to help you navigate crises. However, in this chapter, I'll highlight ordinary people, whom I call heroes, who faced tough challenges and made difficult decisions en route to their destiny – decisions that significantly impacted their lives and others.

Becoming a hero for others during personal challenges involves turning adversity into a catalyst for positive change, both for oneself and for others. It's about transforming personal pain into collective strength and hope.

Each story captures the essence of human strength and faith, reminding us that even in our darkest moments, we can persevere and rise above our circumstances.

***

These heroes haven't put on capes or used superpowers. Nonetheless, their courage and compassion have positively impacted people around the globe.

***

The resilience these heroes exemplify confirms that Hope has no boundary – it's an unwavering commitment to transforming lives, our own and others. I have spoken with each of these remarkable individuals who now bring *healing, opportunities, purpose,* and *empowerment*™ to others, and I am honored to call them friends. Let me now introduce you to the *Heroes of H.O.P.E.* ™.

Cornelia Gibson, LMFT, ED.D.
From Devastating Diagnosis to Destiny

In 2011, Dr. Gibson, a Marriage and Family Therapist, worked two part-time jobs as a single mother of two sons. And after much anticipation, she signed the lease for her weekend private practice. What a significant accomplishment! But her excitement was short-lived. In just a few days, Dr. Gibson began experiencing headaches. She also felt dizzy, and her vision got really bad.

Though needing to work, Dr. Gibson immediately quit one of her part-time jobs because it was no longer safe for her to drive.

Within a week, Dr. Gibson discovered her symptoms' cause – a brain tumor. This medical finding devastated her, leaving her depressed. She was even afraid to sleep out of fear that she might not wake up. She shared, *"Initially, I was scared. I told myself I'm not going to die in my sleep, so I'm never going to sleep."* Dr. Gibson was also concerned about her family, saying, *"I wanted my children and mother to be okay. I worried about how they would manage without me."*

But her perspective changed about a week later. She placed her situation in God's hands – trusting Him to restore her health and enable her to continue her practice. *"I completely turned my health situation over to God and never tried to take it back to fix it myself. My family thought I was in denial of my diagnosis. But I wasn't in denial. I was in faith,"* she remembers. She told me, *"I was okay if the worst happened. I figured God's got me. There's no sense in worrying about something not in your control."*

What an incredible display of faith in our Lord!

Within months of the diagnosis, Dr. Gibson experienced another setback, losing her other part-time job. As a result, she almost lost her house. But Dr. Gibson persevered, and her practice was full within a year. She continued her private practice for four years, serving more people than she'd imagined, sometimes receiving three daily referrals! Then, Dr. Gibson took her private practice in a different direction. She recalls, *"At a conference, God laid it on my heart to open a counseling center called Agape. I had no intention of opening one in the community; I'd planned only to offer private pay services."*

What happened next? The community center flourished, providing mental health training for students at 15 local colleges and universities! And her relentless drive allowed her to offer free services to disadvantaged clients.

However, in July 2021, Dr. Gibson's medical team informed her that she had to have the tumor removed. So, to lift her spirits, Dr. Gibson's family surprised her in a way she won't forget: they gathered five generations in one place and celebrated her birthday! What a special day! But many other blessings followed within a week: Dr. Gibson received a call from The Tamron Hall Show, a local newspaper featured her, and she won a Presidential Medal of Freedom in Health Care Award by the NAACP for her work in her community on mental health.

Dr. Gibson said, *"Receiving all this attention in such a short time helped me understand that my work matters, even without recognition."* She also found a silver lining: *"People will benefit from my testimony,"* Dr. Gibson reflected.

Shortly after receiving these unexpected blessings, Dr. Gibson prepared for brain surgery in December 2021. She carried with her comfort from scripture, saying, *"I went into surgery with 100% peace (Philippians 4:6-7), no stress, no anxiety, and nothing but faith. My pastor and church family prayed for me along the way."*

Thankfully, the surgery proved successful! Shortly after, Dr. Gibson resumed doing what she loves: providing and supervising mental health services for community members.

Today, Agape Counseling Center and Network is a thriving community mental health center in California, serving thousands yearly.

Dr. Gibson credits her tragic diagnosis with the birth of Agape Counseling Center. She says, "*If I had not had the brain tumor, I would have been perfectly fine commuting to my part-time job as a community college counselor, which paid my bills. And I loved my part-time role working in a home for teen mothers. However, God's Agape plan was something much bigger.*"

What lessons did Dr. Gibson learn from her experience? She mentioned two things: "*My decision to overcome adversity taught me that I could do anything if I kept going and that God has more in store for me.*"

When I asked Dr. Gibson what would she tell someone who wants to turn their pain into gain? She replied, "*You can't do it by yourself. Know God. And never give up. It's easy to quit, but rewards for persevering are greater.*"

Find out more at www.agapeccan.org.

Michael Stover

From Drug Addiction to Deliverance

Thanks to God-fearing parents and grandparents, Michael grew up in the church. But around his late 30s, he turned away from his Christian values and started down a path of the unthinkable – he embraced Atheism. Michael said, *"Before I knew what happened, my name changed from Michael to labels that would eventually humiliate me – thief, liar, sex addict, and drug dealer."*

Let's look closer at Michael's downfall.

Michael loved music and enjoyed playing at clubs and other venues. But the trajectory of Michael's life changed with a single decision: accepting illegal drugs from a local club owner. Michael said this about that regrettable moment, *"This decision took me on a downward spiral. I was not living up to my expectations, putting pressure on myself, and putting faith in something else,"* recalls Michael. He continues, *"I was living for myself, for today, with no moral compass."*

Subsequently, Michael became addicted to cocaine. He admitted, *"I'd done so many wrong things to fulfill my desire for the drug."* Michael's drug habit trapped him in an inescapable cycle: finding a job, stealing from his employer to finance his drug addiction, and getting fired by his employer. Michael also began drinking alcohol to numb the high from his drug use. Drugs and alcohol reigned over Michael's life for eight long years.

However, things began to look up for Michael after encountering two individuals.

First, Michael met a fantastic woman who believed in him, but more importantly, she believed in Jesus and the power of prayer to effectuate change in a person's life. *"She had a strong faith,"* Michael fondly recalled.

Michael credits this woman's faith for helping him to reestablish his relationship with God and seek a productive future. Michael still battled demons at this moment, but he felt good about his life.

By the way, Michael married this amazing woman who helped him turn his life around!

Secondly, a store owner who caught Michael stealing from his establishment wanted to press charges against him. However, by God's grace, something unexpected happened: the store owner changed his mind! Michael characterized the store owner's response this way, *"Instead, he felt compassion for me. Knowing that I had a child, this owner wanted me to pay back the money instead of going to court, which could have had significant consequences for me and my child. The man's kindness deeply touched me, showing me I was worth redeeming."*

Afterward, Michael's life began to take a turn for the better. He started regularly attending church, confessed his faults to his wife, and stopped using drugs and alcohol. Michael said this about his newfound enthusiasm, *"I got clean with prayer, not rehab. I was trying to fill a void that Christ could only fill. It was a very hopeless time for me. However, once I gave my life to Him, He lifted me out of my hopelessness and despair."*

Michael explained that God opened his eyes and reacquainted him with his first love – music. As a result of God's blessing,

Michael started his own business as a manager, publicist, and label owner, helping numerous indie artists succeed on airplay and sales charts! Michael is also instrumental in helping his artists gain coverage in significant magazines, sites, and other press outlets.

Not surprisingly, what brings Michael joy is giving back to causes that support homeless and hungry people. He especially delights in helping children with congenital disabilities, who are victims of trafficking, and who have incarcerated parents.

Michael told me, *"Giving back is the most important thing. The more we give, the more He keeps giving. It's truly a blessing, and it all started with the Hope I found in Christ."*

Closing out our interview, I asked Michael how he feels about his life now that he has made it to the other side of his addictions. Smiling, he answered, *"Immensely thankful. Amazed. In awe."*

Find out more at www.mtsmanagementgroup.com.

Bracha Goetz
From Food Addiction to Finding Fulfilment

Bracha grew up in a non-religious Jewish home. By Jewish tradition, she had a Bat Mitzvah, a coming-of-age ceremony for girls turning 12 years old. This unique point in time filled Bracha with a new awareness. Like so many girls her age, Bracha's curiosity about life grew, and she began searching for her purpose for living. Unable to answer these questions satisfactorily, Bracha turned to food, hoping it would fill the void. To her dismay, it didn't. Bracha said, *"Food addictions are a craving for spiritual nourishment, not physical hunger. It's trying to fill a spiritual hole, just as shopping, sexual, or any other addiction does."*

While food provided Bracha with a mind-body connection, it didn't offer any comfort concerning her quest to discover life's meaning. Something was missing. So, in another attempt to find this missing piece, she enrolled at Harvard University to study Psychology.

After enrolling at Harvard, Bracha's struggles with food continued. She said this about her battle with food, *"While at Harvard, I became the sickest I'd been. I looked good on the outside because my extreme dieting and binge eating balanced each other out. However, inside, I felt terrible."* Things got so bad Bracha didn't want to continue living, asking herself, *"What's the point?"*

Bracha received her degree in Psychology, yet she still sought an answer to the elusive question of her life's purpose. Can you picture this? So once again, she turned to education for solace and a solution, enrolling in medical school, but to no avail. Bracha characterized her mental state this way, *"The world seemed gray and drained of color, and I lost Hope. I felt hopeless after reaching the top and finding nothing up there."*

Finally, Bracha's life hit rock bottom during her tenure in Medical School as she ate leftover food in garbage pails. She would later write a book, "Searching for God in the Garbage," recounting what her behavior revealed to her. Bracha said, *"The title is a metaphor for when I searched for my thrown-away heritage. Still, it's deeper than that. It chronicles my behavior and, ultimately, my epiphany."*

So, what did she do about her mental state?

Bracha, who once aspired to become a medical doctor, dropped out of Medical School! Instead of pursuing a medical degree, she explored various religions. To illustrate, Bracha once traveled over 7,000 miles to Israel, much to her parent's dismay. She said, *"My parents thought I was following a cult. However, I was following a deep yearning in my soul that led me to newfound fulfillment."*

Bracha realized she couldn't find a cure for her eating disorder or quest for happiness through her intellectual research. Instead, the solution to end Bracha's obsession with food came to one word – "gratitude." Bracha proclaimed, *"Our whole purpose for living is to express gratitude, and we express gratitude through our relationship with God."*

Today, Bracha lives an abundant life. She's written over 41 picture books that help children grow spiritually, inspiring each uniquely beautiful soul to shine! She also integrates gratitude into her daily life, providing her with all that she longed for: her purpose for living.

Bracha advises us, *"Any moment we are experiencing gratitude is a moment we are not spending being miserable. So try practicing gratitude throughout the day – and over the simplest pleasures – those things you normally overlook and take for granted: opening a window to feel the soft breeze, luxuriously stretching, or slowly savoring a juicy orange."*

Food addictions no longer bound her. Bracha thanks God for her good health, a happy marriage, wonderful children, grandchildren, and the simple things in everyday life.

Bracha closed out our interview with these words of wisdom: *"At any time, a person can bring pleasure into their lives upon waking up and throughout the day. Our world is an amazing garden with so much to be thankful for. So spread joy and thank the source of all these natural pleasures."*

Find out more at www.goetzbookshop.com.

Andrea Wind
From Human Trafficking to Home of Transformation

While searching the internet for a female-oriented organization to support financially, I came across Andrea Wind, the founder of Lighthouse for Life, a nonprofit organization whose mission is to fight to eradicate human trafficking by educating their community and empowering survivors. I instantly connected with her organization.

While Andrea is no longer involved in the organization's day-to-day operations, she was happy to share its history.

Here's Andrea's account of the Lighthouse for Life story:

"I was in church listening to a sermon regarding human trafficking from my pastor when I sensed I would be a part of fighting it. I had yet to learn what that meant because I knew little about it. It took years for human trafficking to reach the public's attention. So

I began to pray and ask God for direction, and over time, He started to bring the pieces together, one by one," Andrea remembers.

Andrea started Lighthouse for Life on a shoestring budget and had no nonprofit operation experience. So, she had to draw from her skills as a schoolteacher and stay-at-home mom. But Andrea did have something more valuable than experience: trust in God. She characterizes her confidence in the Lord, saying, *"Thankfully, God is so good and would bring just the right people into my path at the right time to answer and help me on the step I was on. But He never showed me the next step."*

While initially the approach of having to walk by faith in God and not by sight frustrated Andrea, she began to view it differently, saying, *"I count it a blessing that God didn't show me the big picture ahead of time because I might have backed out after seeing what starting the organization would entail."* One such hurdle was working with governmental agencies. Andrea recounts, *"It was challenging because they didn't have established practices for dealing with trafficking victims nor how to assist me in getting up and running."*

So what did she do?

Andrea persevered and figured things out as she marched forward. She said, *"Over the years, as human trafficking emerged, the organizations and I developed practices that shaped how we could work together."* This learning curve had another upside. Andrea shares, *"During this time of growth, I learned patience and developed my communication and leadership skills."*

In the end, Andrea's diligence paid off – she and other agencies collaborated to spread awareness and support human trafficking victims.

What excited Andrea the most about bringing her vision of Lighthouse for Life to fruition? She said, *"Watching God bring everything together, especially getting their safe house open after years of battling."*

But what Andrea credits as a critical ingredient when tackling an issue like human trafficking is faith.

Andrea reflected, *"Faith is crucial because I have no idea how anyone thinks they could walk into the lion's den of demons around this topic without God and not be completely devoured. The darkness surrounding it is far deeper and darker than I ever realized before getting into it."*

Andrea also recognizes following God's plan for her life to bring the safe house to completion. So, I asked her what advice she would give someone hesitant about following God's plan for their lives.

Andrea gave five suggestions:

1. *Make sure you stay close to God.*

2. *Always have a prayer circle of friends and family around you.*

3. *Journal the journey.*

4. *Stay in your lane.*

5. *Have fun!*

Andrea considers herself a visionary who likes to start things. She ended our interview with this reflection, *"Starting Lighthouse for Life was the most challenging but rewarding initiative. It was an adventure, and I look forward to creating more ministries and organizations."*

Lighthouse for Life has grown tremendously since its inception, educating over 20,000 people (about the seating capacity of Madison Square Garden) about sex trafficking and serving nearly a hundred women since 2021!

Find out more at www.lighthouseforlife.org.

Shelene Bryan

From Skeptical to Skipping

A featured speaker I looked forward to hearing at a Women's Conference had to drop out at the last moment due to an illness. As fate would have it, Shelene Bryan spoke in her place. While she recounted her experience of sponsoring children in Uganda, Africa, through Compassion International – an American child sponsorship and Christian humanitarian aid organization headquartered in Colorado Springs, Colorado – I was all ears since I'd planned to visit Uganda the following month.

Shelene shared the story of a pivotal day in her life while hosting a social event at her home in California. She recounted that a female guest, whom she didn't know, pointed at pictures of the two children she sponsored, Omega, a girl, and Alonis, a boy, hanging on her refrigerator. The lady asked Shelene a startling question: *"You fell for that? How do you know the kids on your refrigerator are real?"* Taken aback, Shelene responded, *"I don't know. I guess I'm just having faith that the money's getting there."*

That question planted a seed of doubt that she couldn't shake. So, what did she do? *"I booked a flight to Uganda to see firsthand where my money was going,"* shared Shelene.

What a bold move!

Shelene then told us about her life-changing trip to Uganda. After landing there, she finally met both her sponsored children! Shelene felt relieved that all her financial contributions positively changed their lives. But she also experienced another emotion: shock at the massive poverty in Uganda, leaving her with a greater appreciation of how God has blessed her. Shelene shared pictures during her talk and told stories of her sponsorship journey. The impact they had on each other's lives moved me.

After Shelene's talk, I rushed to her table to say hello and to receive a copy of her book, "Love Skip Jump," which she gave away for free to people who signed up to sponsor a child.

When I told her I planned to travel to East Africa in a few months, Shelene gave me her book and phone number. While in Africa, I consumed the book in a few days! "Love Skip Jump" takes you on a hilarious and inspiring adventure with Shelene as she recounts how saying yes to God led her, a former Hollywood producer, to the remote parts of Africa and to start a charity organization, Skip1.org.

Shelene said, *"I was not looking to start a charity, but after seeing real starving children in Africa, doing nothing was just not an option."* So she came up with the brilliant idea to challenge people to support the charity out of their excess. Shelene thought, *What if we got everyone on the planet to skip one thing once in their lives – a bottle of water, a manicure, a latte, a pack of gum – and take what they would have spent and donate that money instead to feed starving children?*

Sounds good, right? But intentions and bright ideas are not enough. So, Shelene acted, turning her vision into reality. In her words, *"Jumping is all about taking action. Some of you know exactly what you are called to do. If that's you, now is the time to resolve it."*

But what about those who feel a nudge to do something but hesitate or procrastinate? Shelene shares these words of wisdom based on her own experience, *"I have noticed that many times in my life I have had a moment of epiphany but let that crucial moment of decision pass without taking action. That is typical for many people on the verge of a decision that will change everything, yet they put off making the hard decisions."*

Thankfully, Shelene made the hard decisions and leaped. As a result, Skip1.org supplies food and clean water to children in America and around the world!

Find out more at www.Skip1.org.

Robert Katende
From Suicide to Saving Grace

My husband, Doug, and I visited a museum while vacationing in Uganda, Africa. While Doug chatted with the manager, I browsed a few books to pass the time. Then, one book captured my attention, and I had to buy it.

The book "A Knight Without a Castle: A Story of Resilience and Hope" tells the remarkable story of Robert Katende's hopelessness growing up in poverty in Uganda, Africa. When I began reading the book, I couldn't put it down. Robert's story mesmerized me – I immersed myself in each page, hardly able to wait to see what happened next. Therefore, I felt compelled to feature Robert in this chapter because of all he endured and overcame.

Desperate to interview Robert and get a firsthand account of his life, I contacted him and waited, wondering if I'd get a response. Thankfully, Robert agreed to grant me an interview with him. Our hour-and-a-half conversation confirmed that God ordained our meeting and explained why Robert's humble spirit makes him a hero to many.

When I asked Robert to talk about a dark time in his life, he paused because, according to him, *"There are several."* Then, after much reflection, he shared, *"The one that stands out is when my mom passed away while I was just a boy, around 10. I considered taking my life and attempted but didn't have the means."*

Robert's book tells it this way: *"He had given up on life; it had become meaningless to him...the battle to stay alive had squeezed out every ounce of resilience from his broken spirit, so much so that he had nothing left to keep trying to breathe, sit, stand up and walk. All the things people take for granted."*[1]

So, how did Robert make it through this most challenging time in his life? According to him, it was nothing he did.

He said, *"I know the grace of God is sufficient for each of us. Irrespective of what people go through, I think if you lean on the grace of God, it can sustain you through that."* And who knows this better than Robert? As soon as he overcame one challenge, another lurched around the corner.

Despite the seemingly endless difficulties, Robert pursued his dream of graduating from college and earning a degree in Engineering. But Robert did the unexpected after graduation. Although he got some job offers in his engineering field, Robert was conflicted; should he accept them, or should he follow his heart to help the youth in the Katwe slums? After contemplation, he started the Sports Outreach Ministry (SOM) Chess Academy.

---

1. A knight without a castle: a story of resilience and hope - DC Public Library System. https://link.dclibrary.org/portal/A-knight-without-a-castle--a-story-of-resilence/2w1EnM3c00M/?view=borrow

Robert didn't know it then, but this Academy would be the future saving grace for young people in Katwe, with as many as 400 students gathering under a tent in a single day! What a full-circle moment! He said, *"I thank God that I made what seemed to be a foolish decision then because now there are several degrees coming out of that place."* He continued humbly, *"As I speak right now, we're ministering to over 2500 kids from the slums of Katwe, stretching into Kenya, Rwanda, and the U.S."*

Under Robert's guidance, many students who once floundered flourish – some even graduating with master's degrees from prestigious universities, and others mentoring at the Academy! Robert reflected on his experience, saying, *"I wondered if this could be the reason God enabled me to endure through college, just to know how to lead others there."*

Thank God for Robert – the epitome of a leader and role model!

One of Robert's chess pupils did so well that Disney featured her in "The Queen of Katwe," a Biographical Drama about a 13-year-old girl, Phiona Mutesi, who became a Uganda National Chess Champion under Robert's mentorship. Robert said, *"People ask me how did you go to Disney? I never went to them. They came to us. It was God."*

Robert has a simple life lesson: *"Hope wins! Always be determined to endure and persevere unpleasant circumstances, even when everything may seem to be working against you."*

Robert's insight and jaw-dropping nuggets often left me speechless. He's an incredible leader to learn from.

A master of chess and a father and mentor to many, Robert founded the Robert Katende Initiative. Its mission is to create and set up programs that reach vulnerable children, including disabled kids, and restore Hope and transform lives through chess, one move at a time.

What are Robert's next steps? To build a larger building for the Academy and to expand his programs across the globe.

Find out more at www.robertkatende.org.

Rick and Melissa Hinnant
From Loss to Legacy

While watching one of my favorite television shows years ago, Shark Tank, I noticed a married couple, Rick and Melissa Hinnant, pitching their sewing business to the Shark Tank investors. The backdrop to their business venture resonated with me, especially Melissa's personal story. As a result, I knew I had to share Melissa's journey.

During my research, I discovered that Melissa learned to sew at a young age, but her sewing skills remained dormant until she needed them to jump-start their business. And to her delight, her childhood sewing craft was pivotal to her business success.

Let me highlight some inspiring details about Melissa's heroic story. In 2010, after three years of marriage, Rick and Melissa celebrated their first pregnancy after having difficulty conceiving for over a year. But their joy soon turned to sorrow. [2] Melissa received devastating news during her routine five-month checkup: her unborn daughter would arrive within a day without medical intervention, and she had a low survival possibility. As you can imagine, words can't express Melissa's pain.

So, Melissa underwent surgery at once to save her baby. And it was a success! She and Rick were overjoyed! But Melissa would remain on bed rest until the baby came. During that time, Melissa recalled, *"I became stir-crazy. I felt the need to do something with my hands. I started with a vision to crochet this tiny baby girl's blanket. And thus, began and spurred my desire to sew, sew, sew."*

Melissa remained hospitalized for weeks before going into premature labor. Melissa explained her tragedy this way, *"After doctors could not stop the labor, my baby was born. But she was too immature to survive. Though heart-wrenching and devastating, I truly believe our greatest victory has come from this great tragedy."*

Rick told Melissa they could be bitter, mad, upset, or question God. Instead, he drew a line in the sand, telling her, *"We're not going to do that. We're going to trust God that something good will come out of this. I don't know what it is. We may never know. That's okay. We may never understand, and that's okay, but our stance is, we're going to trust God that something good is going to come."*

Despite the grief, Melissa's sorrow rekindled her passion for sewing. And a year after her emotional trauma, Melissa sewed

---

2. Our Story | Grace & Lace - Grace and Lace.
https://www.graceandlace.com/pages/our-story

her first leg warmers. She also sewed blankets and baby clothes, garnering praise from many people, including her husband, who suggested they sell them online. Her compliments translated to numerous internet orders – so many that they couldn't fill them. Wow! That's not bad for someone just starting a business.

So, how did Rick and Melissa address their challenge?

In 2013, the Hinnants went on the television show Shark Tank. And what happened next far exceeded their expectations and everyone else's. Within five days after their episode aired, their business, "Grace and Lace," a successful women's clothing line, achieved over $1 million in sales, a Shark Tank record!

Because God blessed them with a successful business, they now bless others in ways they never thought possible. Melissa was a missionary as a teen, traveling to many countries and seeing the poorest of the poor.

She says, "When I was 18 or 19, I was in India. We were working in some Mother Teresa homes in Northern India. I had never seen such poverty. I remember writing in my journal that year that I've got to do something more...I thought that meant I'd go off to college, finish college, and come back and spend a significant amount of time here; years, maybe. Never in a million years would I have thought that the Lord would give us a business that would fund the building of orphanages over there, rescuing orphans off the streets, and pulling young girls involved in the sex trade from the border of Nepal!"

What lesson can we learn from Melissa's and Rick's journey? Their story testifies to God's sovereignty: God has absolute power over our situation, can intervene at the right time, and gives us our heart's desires.

Melissa states this about their business, "...*We fully believe that God has given us this business as a platform to inspire others to dream big and beyond their wildest imaginations. We work diligently and do our best but leave the results to God. This is His business, and we are simply the stewards.*"

Melissa and Rick are role models for business owners worldwide; they use their business success to draw lost souls to Christ and leave a legacy for generations.

Find out more at www.graceandlace.com.

Everyday heroes emerge from the test of adversity, transforming personal challenges into platforms to uplift others. Their stories remind us that our struggles can become our strongest testimonies. Let their journeys inspire you to use your unique experiences to empower and light the way for those who follow.

CHAPTER 8

Trading Places

"Count your blessings. Once you realize how valuable you are and how much you have going for you, the smiles will return, the sun will break out, the music will play, and you will finally be able to move forward the life that God intended for you with grace, strength, courage, and confidence." ~Augustine "Og" Mandino

Over the years, my husband and I have had the privilege to visit several African countries: Rwanda, Uganda, Kenya, Egypt, South Africa, Zimbabwe, Zambia, Tanzania, and the coastal island of Zanzibar. Each visit gave us a greater appreciation of the continent. But walking on African soil, our ancestral land, felt surreal, a life-changing experience we treasure.

Regardless of what you see in the Western media, please don't paint Africa with a broad brush – remember, it's a continent, not a country. Like most places, Africa is bittersweet: a mixture of pleasure and pain.

Now let's look at Africa's good and not-so-good:

Africa's Impressive Features and Potential

Goldmine: Africa's loaded with natural resources! It's got 30% of the world's minerals—think gold, diamonds, uranium, and more. And did you know it's got over 60% of the world's untouched farmland?[1]

Nature's Paradise: Africa's landscapes are jaw-droppingly astonishing, from wide-open plains to mind-blowing waterfalls, towering mountains, and lush, green wetlands. Furthermore, the area displays diverse plant life and animals, encompassing many distinctive and vulnerable species, making Africa a top spot for green tourism and sustainable growth.

Green Energy Galore: Africa has deserts for solar panels, rivers for hydropower, and wind-friendly coasts – it's pretty much a green energy goldmine with massive potential. Africa could become a significant player in the clean energy market as the world goes greener.

Tech Titans: Africa's making strides in the tech scene. Take mobile money services, for example – Kenya's M-Pesa is a game-changer, helping people access banking and money services from their phones.

---

1. https://www.unep.org/regions/africa/our-work-africa

Booming Business: Despite its share of problems, Africa's got some of the fastest-growing economies in the world, like Ghana, Ethiopia, and Côte d'Ivoire. Better infrastructure, tech advancements, a rising middle class, and more stable politics fuel this growth. Plus, once the African Continental Free Trade Area gets going, it will be the largest free-trade area in the world by country count, boosting trade within Africa itself.

The Resilience of its People: Africans are renowned for being tough and strong despite hard times. They've dealt with everything from the slave trade to economic troubles, but they keep bouncing back, creating, and transforming their societies. Their vibrant culture is a testament to their adaptability and vigor.

Youth Power: Africa's the youngest continent, with a median age of about 19. This young crowd can significantly boost the world economy in the coming years. If they get the proper education and training, this could profoundly affect productivity and innovation on the continent.

Africa will need serious investment in education, health, governance, and infrastructure to tap into all this potential. But with everything going for it—its vast resources, youthful population, and growing economy—Africa's got a pretty good shot at becoming a big-time economic powerhouse.

Africa's Massive Hardship

Our journey through Africa uncovered a harsh reality about the continent's rampant poverty. The ever-present commercials about starving children don't come close to conveying the overwhelming need in many parts of Africa. My husband and I saw poverty at its peak during our tour through Nairobi, Kenya's slums, where mountains of trash served as a breeding ground for diseases between shacks that families called home. I, the eternal optimist, had no words. Sadly, such dismal living conditions are pervasive in many African countries, with no government aid to mitigate the situation.

***

The resilience of the African people is displayed in their fight for survival, where the absence of safety nets forces them to be inventive in their ways of earning a living. Our translator, Enock, put it this way, "If you don't work, you die."

***

Without government support, such as food stamps, housing, or tuition assistance, their survival largely hinges on their initiative, ingenuity, and adaptability.

Picture this: No soup kitchens, shelters, stimulus packages, paid healthcare, childcare, or free education exist. There is simply no backup plan, and for many, no help from family or friends due to their equally dire circumstances.

My experiences in the Muhanga Village, north of Kigali, Rwanda, profoundly affected my perspective of life in general. I saw an 8-year-old girl named Sipha walking with two younger siblings during school hours and carrying her four-month-old baby brother on her back. Their eyes vividly reminded me of the reality of their existence, displaying determination and resilience.

But stories of such grit were everywhere – from women gracefully balancing fruit bowls or stacks of newspapers on their heads to mothers relentlessly begging for food to feed their babies, to men pushing their bicycles uphill in the heat loaded with goods for sale, earning as little as $2 for a day's labor.

I also watched Tanzanian fishermen who, unlike their American counterparts, do not have the luxury of fishing as a hobby. These fishermen spend hours away from home, casting their nets for survival, their catch crucial for their family's meals.

Finding a way to "make it happen" is a daily theme for many Africans – a normality they navigate with remarkable ambition and discipline. There is no option. A friend in Uganda said, *"Either you make it, or you make it."* Is this sinking in?

***

Here's the reality: Their circumstances are not anomalies, "one-offs," or inconveniences; this is their way of life. But despite our African brothers and sisters' struggles, their adversities don't rob them of their resourcefulness, resilience, creativity, and faith.

***

Instead, they show a spirit of toughness that speaks to the strength of human character when faced with adversity. My African journey has imparted invaluable lessons to me. For example, I discovered the real meaning of wealth, resilience, gratitude, and the value of opportunities. It has instilled in me the belief that every individual has the potential to make a difference in the lives of others, however seemingly small.

After seeing poverty up close, I've also learned to value the intangible over the material. I now think twice about mindless purchasing things I don't need, knowing the dollars I spend buying a dress in the U.S. is enough to feed a family for a month in Africa.

***

> I now recognize that what some consider a "dark time" or "rough patch" in the United States significantly pales compared to the daily struggles in many African nations. And the things we take for granted are what they appreciate most.

***

This realization has prompted me to extend a helping hand, supplying educational opportunities to children, employment training to mothers, feminine hygiene products to women and girls, and water filters for families in Rwandan Villages through my non-profit organization, Hope Springs Africa.

Now Imagine

As a Westerner, reading my sobering account of Africa's widespread poverty may be deeply unsettling, and it should be.

***

Our lives overflow with blessings ingrained in our
daily routines that we don't recognize as such.

***

We have the freedom to dream and the resources to turn those dreams into reality. Despite its flaws, our government provides support systems for those in need.

Take a moment if this narrative of Africa's poverty stirs something in you. Reflect on your life in the United States. Ask yourself: Would you trade places with a person living in poverty in Africa? Would you exchange your comfort, safety nets, and opportunities for their daily struggle for survival?

The answer will likely be 'No.' That 'No' is born not out of fear or disdain but of an awakened realization of the many privileges we often take for granted. That 'No' is a moment of gratitude, a prayer of thanksgiving for your daily blessings.

But let's not let it end in gratitude. Let that 'No' also inspire you to take action. While we can't all go to Africa and change people's circumstances, we can make a difference in other ways. By supporting local and international organizations working towards poverty eradication, spreading awareness about global poverty, and becoming responsible global citizens, we can contribute to change.

***

> As we look out of our windows into our secure, comfortable lives, let's reflect on how good we have it. And when we want to complain, let's think twice, knowing someone would love to trade places.

***

Let's remember Sifa. Then, let that image be our call to gratitude and action.

Remember, we have the power not just to count our blessings but to be a blessing in the lives of others, even in the midst of our challenges.

TRADING PLACES 103

Sifa and her siblings

CHAPTER 9

Marching Orders

"While there's life, there is Hope." ~Stephen Hawkin

Life is full of twists and turns, highs and lows. There's no doubt about it. The good news is that we have a choice in navigating them. Do we complain and crumble, or do we listen and learn? Do we fall apart or fall to our knees? Do we meet trouble head-on or try to hide from it, wishing it would work itself out?

In earlier chapters, I've given inspiration, encouragement, and action steps to help you overcome life's most profound disappointments and demanding challenges. I've also invited you to look at Hope differently – not just what it means but what it offers – **h**ealing, **o**pportunities, **p**urpose, and **e**mpowerment.™

Here's a summary of what we covered with a call to action:
  Chapter 1: *Searching for Answers*
  - It is natural and beneficial to question the fairness of life's trials.

- Asking "Why" provides self-discovery and personal growth.

- Hope gives you comfort and confidence during challenging times.

Chapter 2: *Sending Out an "SOS"*
- Your SOS isn't a crisis or a test; it's a season of learning.

- Like the changing seasons of nature, our lives also undergo cycles of challenges and growth.

- Endure and embrace the full spectrum of life's experiences.

Chapter 3: *Staying Afloat*
- Don't allow life's challenges to conquer you.

- Stay afloat by employing simple but life-changing strategies.

- Cling to Hope to keep you on course.

Chapter 4: *Pressing Forward*
- Press forward, even when the path seems daunting and unclear.

- Progress doesn't always come in leaps and bounds but in small, steady steps.

- Celebrate each stride, knowing they bring you closer to your destiny.

Chapter 5: *Turning Your Pain into Gain*
- Find the bright side of bad situations.

- With pain comes healing and growth.

- Overcoming your challenges inspires others.

Chapter 6: *Reaching Your Destiny*
- Walk out God's purpose for your life.

- Allow your choices, passions, and determination to shape your destiny.

- Dare to envision a future filled with limitless possibilities.

Chapter 7: *Empowering Lives*
- Hope breeds empowerment.

- Our stories have meaning.

- You are the hero someone needs.

Chapter 8: *Trading Places*
- Count your blessings.

- Commit to improving the lives of those in need.

- Start making a difference today.

As I conclude this guidebook on Hope, my heart is overflowing with gratitude for the transformative power of Hope in my life and for the reminder that it is not a distant destination but a powerful force within us. Remember, we can either let our challenges capsize us or catapult us toward our destiny.

I now extend a heartfelt call to action to you:

- Embrace Hope in all its forms – yourself, others, and the future. When life's storms threaten to overwhelm you, remember that Hope will guide you to calmer shores.

- Share your story and be a beacon of Hope for others; you never know how your resilience can inspire someone else to keep going.

- Cultivate an "attitude of gratitude," for it is the fertile ground where Hope blossoms.

- Give to others because it enriches both the lives of the recipients and the givers, fostering a cycle of kindness that can lead to a brighter and more interconnected world.

Remember that every small act of kindness, every word of encouragement, and every expression of empathy can make a difference in someone's life.

I invite you to go forth from this closing chapter with your heart full of Hope and your spirit alight with the knowledge that you hold the key to transforming lives, including your own.

Thank you for joining me on this journey. May your path be illuminated forever, and Hope, strength, gratitude, and joy be your constant companion.

And if this book helped and inspired you, please write a review where you bought it to help more people find it. You can also share your thoughts and Unwavering Hope stories with me at rhonda@rhondamincey.com.

Challenging and cheering you on, with love,
Rhonda

About the Author

Rhonda G. Mincey

Rhonda Mincey, M.Ed., is the *"Giver of H.O.P.E.™."* She helps other people elevate.™ As the Chief Inspirational Officer of Great Success, L.L.C., she supports women in midlife to tell their stories on pages and stages through her Women Who P.O.P.™ – Prosper on Purpose™ membership.

Rhonda is an award-winning mentor, world traveler, international speaker, humanitarian, success coach, poet, and author who enjoys traveling abroad.

Rhonda's books, *Unbridled Dreams: Change Your Mindset, Achieve Your Goals, and Live the Best Story of Your Life*, and *A Girl's Guide to Being Great*, are highly acclaimed.

Believing to whom that much is given, much is required, Rhonda donates a portion of her revenue to support women and girls in developing countries.

Rhonda also founded the nonprofit Hope Springs Africa to provide clean drinking water, educational supplies, and feminine hygiene products to people in villages in Rwanda, Africa.

When Rhonda isn't on a plane, stage or beach, you might find her writing, reading inspirational books, listening to music, or spending time with family and friends. To connect or consult with Rhonda, visit www.rhondamincey.com

Also By

Rhonda G. Mincey

www.ingramcontent.com/pod-product-compliance
Lightning Source LLC
LaVergne TN
LVHW051600080426
835510LV00020B/3059